# 1 MONTH OF
# FREE
# READING

## at

## www.ForgottenBooks.com

By purchasing this book you are eligible for one month membership to ForgottenBooks.com, giving you unlimited access to our entire collection of over 1,000,000 titles via our web site and mobile apps.

To claim your free month visit:

www.forgottenbooks.com/free870597

ISBN 978-0-265-58286-2
PIBN 10870597

This book is a reproduction of an important historical work. Forgotten Books uses state-of-the-art technology to digitally reconstruct the work, preserving the original format whilst repairing imperfections present in the aged copy. In rare cases, an imperfection in the original, such as a blemish or missing page, may be replicated in our edition. We do, however, repair the vast majority of imperfections successfully; any imperfections that remain are intentionally left to preserve the state of such historical works.

# THE
# ASHBURIAN

# ASHBURY COLLEGE
## OTTAWA

VOL. XXIV          MICHAELMAS          No. 1
1940

# THE
# ASHBURIAN

# ASHBURY COLLEGE
## OTTAWA

VOL. XXIV                    MICHAELMAS                    No. 1
1940

To the High Commissioner in Canada for the United Kingdom, Sir Gerald Campbell, K.C.M.G., D.C.L., LL.D., this issue of The Ashburian is respectfully dedicated.

# TABLE OF CONTENTS

# TABLE OF CONTENTS (Junior)

# Board of Governors

Shirley E. Woods, Esq.
*Chairman*

H. S. Southam, Esq.
*Deputy Chairman*

# The Staff

---

### Headmaster

N. M. ARCHDALE, M.A.,
The Queen's College, Oxford

### Housemaster and Senior Master

A. D. BRAIN, B.A. (Toronto)
Sometime Scholar of Exeter College, Oxford

### Assistant Housemaster

H. M. PORRITT, M.A. (Bishop's)

### Headmaster Junior School

G. J. K. HARRISON, M.A.,
Trinity College, Oxford

REV. W. S. TIGGES, B.Sc. (Hailan)
M.Sc. (Upsala)
Ph. D. (Halle-Wittenberg)
B.D. (Heidelberg and Muenster)

G. S. B. MACK, (Dublin)
Sometime Scholar and Senior Moderator
Trinity College, Dublin.

E. D. HARRISON, B.A. (London)

D. L. POLK, B.A. (Dartmouth)

R. A. SYKES

MRS. E. B. HUNTER

MISS E. BARKER

### Dietitian and Nurse Matron

MISS F. MORONI, R.N.

### Assistant Nurse Matron

MISS H. A. MacLAUGHLIN, R.R.C., R.N.

### Bursar

F. HUNTER

### Secretary

MISS D. LYON

### Organist

H. HUGGINS, B.A., LL.B.

### Cadet Corps Instructor

SERGEANT-MAJOR COX, ex-R.C.D.

### Physical Training Instructor

W. R. C. McADAM

# School Officers

### Captain of the School
C. R. Burrows

### Captain of the Boarders
G. D. Hughson

### Prefects

J. A. Smart　　　　　G. W. Green　　　　　J. A. MacGowan

A. M. M. Curry

### House Monitors

G. R. Goodwin　　　　　G. S. Fisher　　　　　D. P. Phillips

### Cadet Corps

*Corps Leader*

Cadet Major G. W. Green

*Second-in-Command*

Cadet Captain C. R. Burrows

*Corps Quartermaster*

Cadet Lieut. H. M. Hughson

*Platoon Commanders*

Cadet Lieut. G. D. Hughson　　　　　Cadet Lieut. A. M. M. Curry

*Cadet Sergeant-Major*

J. P. Thomas

*Cadet Quartermaster-Sergeant*

B. P. Mordy

*First Aid*

Cadet Lieut. R. D. Viets

### Games Captains

*Rugby*　　　　　*Hockey*　　　　　*Cricket*

C. R. Burrows　　　J. A. MacGowan　　　R. B. Bailey

*Soccer*

R. B. Bailey

### Games Vice-Captains

*Rugby*　　　　　*Hockey*　　　　　*Cricket*

J. P. Thomas　　　C. R. Burrows　　　C. R. Burrows

*Soccer*

G. W. Green

### House Captains

*Connaught*　　　　　　　　　*Woollcombe*

A. M. M. Curry　　　　　　　　　C. R. Burrows

# Ashburian Staff
## 1940 - 1941

---

### Editor-in-Chief
H. M. Porritt, Esq., M.A.

### Editor
G. W. Green

### Assistant Editors

G. D. Hughson                                    H. M. Hughson

#### News
E. P. Newcombe
M. Barnes
D. N. Farson

#### Sports
H. B. Heath
H. J. MacDonald
R. T. Holmes

### Advertising Managers
T. W. Spafford                                   A. M. M. Curry

# The Ashburian Junior
### in which is incorporated
# Abinger Hill Magazine
### Editor
J. N. Turner

### Assistant Editors
D. L. Matthews                                   M. Arlen

**SIR GERALD CAMPBELL, K.C.M.G.**

December 10, 1940.

Dear Sir,

My first thought was that I could not mention the word "happy" in connection with Christmas or the New Year at this time of world crisis, but that did not seem quite fair, so I summoned a second thought and it came up smiling. It reminded me that a most interesting liaison has been established during the past six months between the Old World and the New. How long the Old World is going to continue as such I do not know—a miserable person called Goering said even before the war broke out, that whatever happened Europe would be in ruins—nor do I know how long this Continent is going to be called the New World; that is a minor matter—what is important is that the Old has its offering to make of experience and tradition and the New can and does contribute enthusiasm and an expansiveness which is denied to many who live within narrower, more cramping confines.

So what more profitable arrangement can there be than that on the campus and in the class rooms of Ashbury College there should mingle unembittered representatives of the Old and the New World, and how reasonable it is to wish and expect that you will all be happy at this season and in the year to come, as you absorb (possibly unrealized by you at the time) the mutual benefits of this encounter.

Good luck to all of you; to Abinger Hill boys awaiting their first Canadian Christmas, and to Ashbury boys who are going to get an added kick out of the happiness they are giving their friends from across the sea.

Yours sincerely,

Gerald Campbell.

**THE HEADMASTER**

**ASHBURY COLLEGE**
ROCKCLIFFE PARK
OTTAWA

N. M. ARCHDALE, M.A.
HEADMASTER

December 10, 1940.

Dear Sir,

I was the more ready to comply with your request for a letter about our guests from England, as it gave me an opportunity to emphasize an aspect of this migration of boys from one country to another which is far too frequently forgotten.

I refer to the broadening of outlook obtained by actually living in a country other than one's own. Before long these boys will probably be returning home and will provide, in company with those who have gone to the other Dominions and to the United States of America, a priceless leaven of knowledge of other parts of the world.

When one looks around and sees the chaos in the world at the present time, and when one remembers that this was caused to a great extent not only by ignorance on the part of the people of one country about the way of life, customs and thought of the people of other countries, but by a refusal to make any attempt to get to know these things, the more people from one country who can be persuaded to live for a time in another country, the more in fact that a system of interchange of citizens can be developed in the world, the more chance there is of peace and goodwill.

With that point in view, it is very pleasing to be able to say at the end of this first term of the temporary amalgamation of Abinger Hill School with Ashbury College, that both groups have shown a readiness to appreciate and understand each other's point of view, which means that the experiment is proving an unqualified success.

In conclusion, I should like to express in
print a hearty welcome to all our visitors, to
assure them that we will do all we can to make
their stay both pleasant and profitable, and also
to thank very sincerely all the kind friends who
have come to our help with such generosity, par-
ticularly with hospitality, for the Abinger boys.

Yours sincerely,

*Nicholas. M. Archdale.*

ASHBURY COLLEGE
ROCKCLIFFE PARK
OTTAWA

December 10, 1940.

Dear Sir,

Having been generously allowed a page of
the Ashburian, I take this opportunity to thank
publicly the Governors of Ashbury and the Headmaster
for the fact that Abinger Hill School is here under
Ashbury's hospitable roof. This fact is, in itself,
the result of much generosity of pocket, and kindness of spirit.

I understand that Sir Gerald Campbell has
been good enough to accept this issue of the Magazine in his name, and that he is writing a Foreword
for it. I am glad to have the chance here to thank
Sir Gerald for the infinite trouble he has taken on
our behalf since we arrived in Canada early in July,
the more especially because no man can be carrying
a heavier burden of responsibility and hard work
than he is himself at the present time.

Next I am glad to be able to write a
message of appreciation to all Ashbury—because it is
the happiest possible thing that the mixing of the two
Schools has taken place with such equable blending.
This blending is due entirely—and I use the ad-
verb intentionally—to Ashbury, which has received
us all with so much helpfulness and friendliness.
In every part of school life—and we must not forget
the kindness of the members of the Staff who gave
up so much of their summer holidays to help us
"settle"—Ashbury has shown more thoughtful kindness
in all sorts of small ways than I am able to detail
without appearing fulsome. Perhaps it is best to say
that none of us will ever forget it.

There are, of course, many problems connected with evacuation that present difficulties to
those who now, throughout the Empire, are offering

the hospitality of their homes.  These difficulties,
and ours, are, I believe, the theme of the Senior
Editorial.  Life cannot always be wholly easy, even at
ten, being separated from the things which ten years
of life have made dear and familiar, but all whom
we have met over here have done everything to smooth
the way.

        Finally, I should like to thank you, Sir,
for your gesture in incorporating our Magazine in
the Ashburian Junior, and allowing its continuity in
your pages.

        We wish continued and deserved success to
Ashbury, and thank you from our hearts.

                    Yours very sincerely,

                    James Harrison.

# EDITORIAL

**W**HAT'S in an Editorial? The Editorial of a School Magazine must concern itself, naturally, with the most important event in the School since the last issue of the magazine went to press. This Editorial, therefore, will concern itself with the adoption by Ashbury of Abinger Hill—an event of great significance and, possibly, the most important event in the School's history.

Abinger Hill was founded in September 1927, and has flourished ever since as one of England's well-known Preparatory Schools. It is to be regretted that the exigencies of the war necessitated its evacuation to alien shores. But with the passing of each day the alien firelight burns ever brighter with a stronger flame, and we can only hope that "from the midst of cheerless gloom," they have indeed passed "to the bright, unclouded day."

"Actions and Reactions;" so with Abinger. But if there has been friendly reactions on this side of the water it has been prompted by friendly actions on the part of those whom we now welcome to Ashbury. The boys of Abinger Hill know, fortunately, both how to give and how to receive. And they have given a great deal. They have shown adaptability, a genuine desire to get on with the other fellow, good will, and, we think, a real liking for our country.

But as they have given, so they have received—and they have received much; holidays, winter clothing and, above all, the kindness and hospitality of Canadian homes. The fact that the Abinger boys are always "asked back," that so many are guests of friends of Ashbury, speaks for itself. Kindness, such kindness, it is, of course, almost impossible to repay. But the boys of Abinger Hill can reciprocate in one way—by never forgetting their own School and its traditions, our School and her traditions, their country, their King, and their faith.

W E regret, with all who knew him, the death at Ardvar, Rockcliffe, of Mr. G. E. Fauquier who, for so many years, had been a great friend to Ashbury.

Mr. Fauquier's part in Canada's story is too well known for comment here, but for the interest of those who are new to the School, it might not be inappropriate to recall the most outstanding facts of his life. We owe, in large measure, the Halifax docks to him; the development of the Grand Trunk Pacific in Western Ontario was inspired by his organizing ability, and his direction of salvage work and shipbuilding on the east coast helped us, more than a little, to win the first great battle against the Hun.

To Mrs. Fauquier and her children we offer our deepest sympathy. No family has been more intimately connected with Ashbury. Mr. Fauquier was a former Chairman of our Board of Governors; four of his sons have been Head Prefects; Gilbert, Adam, John and David, and so we feel an especial pride in the association of the name of Fauquier with Ashbury. If it is a credit to us that we have had four Fauquiers as Heads of the School, it but reflects on their father, and if we have lost the father's kindly advice and helping hand, we know that we will always retain the memory of a very charming gentleman.

# SCHOOL NOTES

S INCE the end of last term we have been deprived of several of the Staff. Mr. Johnson, who had been on the Staff for some years, and Senior Master for the last two, has left, and, as noted, in the last issue, he is now attached to G.H.Q., with the rank of captain. Mr. Wood has left to receive his commission as a lieutenant in the G.G.F.G. Mr. McLeish, who had been with us for two years, has joined up with the R.C.A.F. and has been transferred to Brandon, Man. Mr. Elder and Dr. Kohr also left last June.

We welcome to the school this year an unusually large addition to the Staff. The present Headmaster of the Junior School is Mr. James Harrison who brought the whole of Abinger School to Canada this July. He is now engaged in teaching languages and English in the Junior and Middle Schools, as well as Greek to some in the Senior School. After having received his School Certificate at Shrewsbury, he entered Trinity College, Oxford, where, after studying Classics and English Literature, he received his B.A. and M.A., and where he rowed in his college eight. He taught at Horris Hill School for a year, and afterwards did some teaching and studying in New York. Then, in 1927 he was appointed Headmaster of Abinger Hill School.

Dr. William Tigges is engaged in teaching science to the Senior School. Having received his primary training in Stockholm, Sweden, he attended Hailan College and there received his B.Sc. Degree. He then received his M.Sc. at Upsala, and two years later wrote his Ph. D. dissertation at Halle-Wittenberg. A year afterwards he received his B.D. at Heidelberg, where he studied Social and Natural Science. in 1929 he was ordained a minister of the United Church of Canada, having come to this country two years previously. After a long and varied career as a teacher and minister he finally settled down in Ottawa, where he entered the staff of the Department of Labour to write a memorandum on Sociology, and finally came, this term, to Ashbury.

Mr. G. S. B. Mack is teaching languages and history in the Senior School When he received his matriculation in Dublin he entered Trinity College, and there received his Double Senior Moderatorship, for which he specialized in history and classics. He played on the Irish Team for the Davis Cup and also represented Ireland on her Badminton Team. He was also All-England Badminton Champion, winning matches in both singles and doubles. For nine years he was Headmaster of Sandford Park School in Dublin, and after resigning this position he came to Canada. We will appreciate greatly his coaching us in badminton and tennis in the terms to come, and we feel sure that he will turn out some fine teams.

Mr. E. D. Harrison is now teaching mathematics to the Senior and Middle Schools. He attended Munro College in Jamaica for ten years, and having received a Scholarship he entered University College, London. There he received his B.A. in mathematics. Then he went back to Munro College and remained there as a master until this summer.

Mr. D. L. Polk, who teaches languages and history to the Junior School, comes from the United States. After he attended Windsor School he entered Dartmouth College, N.H., and majoring in Sociology and English, he received his B.A. For one year he taught at Yardley Court School in England, and then he came back to America and subsequently to Ashbury.

Mr. R. A. Sykes is with us for one term in the capacity of language master, teaching in the Junior School. He went to Bickley Hall, and then to Seven Oaks School, and then he became a master in Upcott House School. After a year in that position he became a Housemaster in Abinger Hill. When he came to Canada this summer as an Abinger Master, he was in charge of two hundred girl refugees. Unfortunately, at the end of this term he expects to be leaving to re-enter the R.A.F.

Miss E. Barker takes the whole of the Pre-Prep School (our newly started kindergarten) in the morning, and also takes some of the Junior School classes in the afternoon. She was first educated at Lawnswood High School, Leeds, and from there she entered the Leeds Hospital and received two years training in the childrens' ward and one year in the general ward. Later she became a tutor for private families. She had a private school of her own in Madeira for three years and subsequently did some more tutoring before she came to Ashbury this year.

We also welcome to the school Mr. R. McAdam who was a basketball star at Glebe and who now takes us in Gym, Sergeant-Major Cox who has taken over the Cadet Corps, and Miss H. A. MacLaughlin who is assisting Miss Moroni in her duties as Matron.

------------------

At the funeral of the late Mr. G. E. Fauquier, the School was represented by the Headmaster, and the Captain of the School, C. R. Burrows. A wreath was sent in Ashbury's name.

------------------

It was with deep regret that we learnt of the death of Major F. E B. Whitfield, M.B.E. Mr. Whitfield was a member of the Staff for many years, but since he left Ashbury he had been in considerable ill health. Mr. Whitfield will be remembered for his great interest in games at Ashbury, as well as for his ability to teach classics. To his widow and to his children we offer our deepest sympathy. Mr. Porritt and the Captain of the School represented Ashbury at the funeral, and a wreath was sent in the name of all of us.

We also regret to record the death of Mr. Lou Coté, who was for many years responsible for the successes of the Senior Rugby Team.

We should like to offer cur congratulations to Mr Archdale upon his recovery from the operation he underwent th:s summer.

---

This year the school has more than doubled its numbers, and on top of that we welcome Abinger Hill School of Surrey, England. As the Editorial has dealt at some length with this addition to our numbers, we will content ourselves with prophesying that their stay with us will be mutually pleasant.

---

We congratulate Mr Brain on the second addition to his family. Victoria (Vicky) has not been seen much as yet, but neither, for that matter, has she been heard overmuch.

The Senior School would like to thank the Headmaster for the Saturday night dances this term. This new form of recreation is exceedingly popular, and the Senior House more than welcomes this variation in week-end routine.

At the beginning of the term, Dr. Woollcombe paid a visit to the school and in a brief address welcomed the new boys.

The pre-Preparatory school, under Miss Barker, has flourished and now boasts twelve members. The small desks and chairs in what used to be Room "G" afford some amusement to the more august Seniors.

A Science Club has been organized under the supervision of Dr. Tigges. There are twenty-five members, who have elected their own President, and they meet twice a week in their free time. The purpose of the club is to study and discuss practical experiments in elementary science.

At the time of the appeal of the Ottawa Community Chests, Mr. Sparks spoke to the school, and on Nov. 6, Mr. Atkinson, the Principal of Glebe Collegiate, spoke to the boys on the significance of Poppy Day.

Early in November we were privileged to hear a lecture from the Rev. Howard Green. This lecture on the Columbia Mission, which does such notable work in British Columbia, was illustrated by some of the most remarkable coloured films that your Editors have ever seen. It was an evening not only of entertainment but of instruction.

On Nov. 25, Mr. J. M. Humphrey gave an illustrated lecture on the romance and beauty of the Maritimes. This lecture, too, was highly appreciated.

We commend Tony Bidwell for his initiative in organizing a Childrens' Dog and Gold Fish show in order to help the Red Cross. The prizes were donated by friends, and the complete proceeds sent to the organization.

The school was recently paid a visit by Sir Cedric Hardwicke. One member of your editorial staff has been jittery ever since!

Towards the middle of November, a Mock Parliament was held in the gymnasium which, incidently, lends itself much more suitably to the purpose than did the old Assembly Hall. Instead of the desks facing the Speaker, chairs can be placed in such a position that the seating represents exactly that in the House of Commons. As yet no new elections have been held in the School, and Boutin remains Prime Minister, with Howe leader of His Majesty's Most Loyal Opposition. After the usual question period, two main bills were debated; one concerning the incorporation of Great Britain into the joint Canadian-American Defence Board, and the other—prognosticating, strangely enough, an actual bill in the Dominion House of Commons—concerning the necessity of increasing the number of Canada's warships. Debate was not, on the whole, good, but more spirited than before. A new election is almost certain early next term.

Mrs. Archdale gave her usual party for the Boys on Hallowe'en, and on many other occasions the Headmaster and Mrs. Archdale have entertained various Boarders and Day Boys.

We are pleased to see another Cavendish at Ashbury this year. Timothy Hunloke, who is in the pre-Preparatory, is the son of the former Lady Anne Cavendish. It will be recalled that Lord Charles Cavendish entered Ashbury as a Boy in 1917, while his father, the Duke of Devonshire, was Governor General of Canada.

Last, but not least in the School Notes, we welcome Georgina, one of the most lovable characters ever to invade these halls of learning. Georgina, we should remark, is Mr. G. J. K. Harrison's most petted possession. She is a pedigree Great Dane with beautiful black and white markings, and eyes which speak for themselves. A lady of great appeal and charm, she appeared on her third birthday, November 28, wearing bows in School colours. Her father's name is lost in the pages of antiquity, but we do know that her mother was called Prudence.

# CHAPEL NOTES

A S is customary at Ashbury, most of the Sunday morning services have been conducted by the Headmaster. On several occasions, however, guest preachers have assisted at the service. As is mentioned in the report of the unveiling of the Harry F. Wright Memorial, on November 10, the School was addressed by the Rev. L. S. Nesbitt. Previous to that date Mr. Brain and Mr. G. J. K. Harrison preached at matins.

Dr. Woollcombe has again this year celebrated Holy Communion in the Chapel, where a large number of communicants have received the Sacrament.

On Remembrance Day, November 11, a service was held in memory of the Armistice, and of those Old Boys who fell in the War of 1914-1918. In the past we have not held—as a rule—services in the chapel because the Corps, comprising most of the School, has paraded with the parent regiment, the Governor General's Foot Guards. This year, however, we were denied this privilege, as the G.G.F.G. is away training for overseas service. The Headmaster conducted the service, and Goodwin read the memorable lesson from Ecclesiasticus, "Let us now praise famous men . . ."

Goodwin has read the Sunday lessons this term, and a marked improvement is to be noticed in his delivery.

With everybody's attention focused on the war, our prayers have been asked repeatedly for those Old Boys now overseas, and it has been suggested that the School's prayer for them be printed here. This prayer, incidentally, is the one said in T.C.S., Port Hope, and we are indebted to Mr. Ketchum for allowing us to adopt the prayer for our own use—the common prayer, though the words may vary, of all schools.

"O Almighty God, who art wiser than the children of men and overrulest
"all things to their good, hold, we beseech Thee, in Thy keeping all who
"have gone forth to battle from this School: watch over those that are
"missing: comfort and protect those that are in the hands of the enemy.
"Be with them in the hour of danger, strengthen them in the hour of
"weakness, sustain and comfort them in the hour of sickness or of death.
"Grant that they may be true to their calling and true always to Thee,
"and make both them and us to be strong to do our duty in Thy service,
"through Jesus Christ our Lord. *Amen.*"

On Sundays Mrs. Wittaker has played at both services.

**THE CHAPEL**

Mr. Huggins, playing our accompaniments on week-days, continues to delight all of us, and the following brief description of the organ which Mr. Huggins has kindly written for the Ashburian, was prompted by a remark overheard in the halls when a Junior wondered what on earth the organist kept doing with his feet during the playing of the morning hymn. It occurred to the Editors, therefore, that it would be a good thing if Mr. Huggins could explain briefly what an organ is and describe generally how it is played. We reproduce below what Mr. Huggins wrote for us.

"As many boys have wondered just why the School Organist appears to act in an eccentric manner when he plays the Chapel organ, the following words of explanation may prove of interest.

"When you look at our Casavant Chapel organ you see merely a large number of metal pipes above a desk-like structure, known as the console. Two rows of playing keys are provided, one to be used by the feet only, and one by the hands only. Just above the latter is a small row of ivory rocking tablets known as "stops;" whose function is just that very thing, to stop or shut off any given row of pipes from sounding.

"When a key is depressed by the organist, a current of air, originating in a blower located in the basement of the Chapel, is permitted to pass through a valve into a pipe where it sets up a vibration at a fixed rate, dependent upon the size of the pipe and the pressure of the air current in question. The vibration thus set up reaches our ears in the form of a sound wave, and we call it a musical tone.

"Obviously, an organist is bound to appear to be a busy person, because he is, at the same time, usually employing both hands and both feet, besides the other faculties of sight and hearing. Every effort is made to cut down waste motion to the minimum, as it is only fatiguing to the player and a distraction to the spectator.

"The metal pipes visible in our Chapel organ are known as diapasons, .from the Greek "dia", through, and "pas", all. That is, the diapason tone runs through the whole gamut or tonal range of the organ, from deepest bass to highest treble. This so-called diapason tone is the only true legitimate tone of the organ, examples of it being found in the earliest known interest. All other qualities of tone are merely imitative of orchestral instruments, such as the flute, reed, string and percussion families.

THE SCHOOL

"One further query remains to be answered. Not all the visible pipes of our organ, or of most organs for that matter, function. Certain of them are dummy, and are provided only to make a symmetrical pattern, pleasing to the eye. The real pipes are behind. In conclusion, we should not forget that the bellows in the organ are the most essential part of its mechanism. Without bellows to push the air through the pipes, no organ can work. In earlier days, these were inflated by hand, but now this is done by electricity, and unless the switch by the organ is pushed, no sound will be forthcoming."

**THE HARRY F. WRIGHT MEMORIAL**

# MEMORIAL TABLET UNVEILED

A N interesting ceremony took place in the Chapel at matins on Sunday, November 10, when the memorial plaque to the memory of the School's second Headmaster was dedicated and unveiled. The tablet, a photograph of which appears on the opposite page, is a gift of the Old Boys of the School. It will be recalled that last year's Christmas issue of the Ashburian was dedicated to the memory of Mr. Wright. Tribute to the late Headmaster's memory was eloquently paid by Dr. Woollcombe at the service, and after his few remarks, the Founder, and the Rev. L. H. Nesbitt, who preached the sermon, proceeded to the back of the Chapel, where the tablet has been placed.

The acting President of the Old Boys' Association, Cargill Southam, then pulled the cord which raised the Union Jack, and the memorial was dedicated by Dr. Woollcombe to the glory of God and in loving memory of Harry Frederick Wright.

In addition to Cargill Southam, many other Old Boys availed themselves of the opportunity of paying their respects to a man whom they had all known as friend. Among those who were noticed in the congregation were Lieutenant H. A. Fauquier, R.C.R., Lieutenant David Fauquier, Lieutenant Hugh M. Baker, Gilbert Fauquier and Donald Maclaren.

# OLD BOY NOTES

## WITH THE SERVICES

O N Sept. 26th, Angus MacDonald, Minister of the Navy, announced officially
that the Canadian armed merchant cruiser, *Prince Robert*, captured the
German express cargo ship, *Weser*, off the Mexican Pacific coast. The
*Weser*, of 9,180 tons had as a cargo over 19,000 barrels of oil.

We congratulate most sincerely C. T. Beard, who was in command of the *Prince
Robert* when he wirelessed Naval Headquarters of the seizure. Climaxing a long
game of watching and waiting, Commander Beard brought the *Prince Robert* along-
side the German freighter before she had time to scuttle herself, and a prize crew took
command of the captured vessel. As far as is known, this is the Canadian Navy's
biggest and richest haul, and we are proud to remember that Commander Beard is
an old Ashburian.

We regret to hear that Flying Officer W. F. Tudhope, son of Squadron Leader
J. H. Tudhope of World War fame, was reported missing on Aug. 12th. He had
previously been awarded the D F.C. for valour in night bombing raids over Germany.
He is now presumed lost.

The second of Ashbury's Old Boys in the R.A.F. to give his life for his country,
was Flying Officer Frederick Lambart who was killed in an aircraft accident in
England on Aug. 13th. Born in Ottawa, he joined the R.A.F. in 1937 and was
mentioned in dispatches as one of the heroes of the Heligoland engagement soon
after the beginning of the war.

Lieut.-Commander Jack Hose, son of Rear Admiral Hose, has been recently appointed commanding officer of the local division of the Royal Canadian Naval Volun-
teer Reserve. He has been connected with the R.C.N.V.R. since 1923, and is well
qualified for his new post. He succeeds Lieut. T. D'Arcy McGee.

James Hamilton has joined the Royal Canadian Regiment and is at present on
service in England.

"Mike" Wood, who is holding a commission overseas in the R.C.A.S.C., is about
to train as a pilot officer in the R.A.F. His older brother, until recently a Master
here, has left Ottawa with the 1st Battalion of the G.G.F.G.

John Lewis has joined the 25th battery as a gunner.

Sub-Lieut. D. K Edwards has arrived in England for training at a Royal Naval
establishment.

We should like to correct our statement in the last issue that George Hyman
was in the Black Watch. He is with the 2nd Battalion, Victoria Rifles of Canada.

On November 25th, Eric Beardmore arrived back in Canada on leave, convalescing from wounds he received when his plane was shot down. A member of the First Fighter Squadron of the R.C.A.F., he came down over the Thames in a battle with German fighter planes. Hit by machine-gun bullets, he bailed out and landed safely in the water, to be rescued by the Royal Navy.

On the same day that Beardmore arrived back in Montreal, Pilot Officer Art Snell arrived in England, one of the first graduates of the great Empire Air Training Scheme. That night, in one of the regular broadcasts of With the Canadian Troops in England, Bob Bowman interviewed Snell and together they recalled Ashbury and the good times they had had here. Snell left us in 1924.

We have just mentioned Snell. At the time of going to press we have heard of his arrival in England, and his being very much On Active Service within a few hours. We reproduce below the account published in the Ottawa *Journal*.

### A. SNELL OF OTTAWA IN ATTACK 48 HOURS AFTER ARRIVAL

Helps Bomb Boulogne, Nazi Invasion Base.
(By Ross Munro, Canadian Press War Correspondent.)

Somewhere in England, Dec. 11.--Some members of the first class of Canadians graduated in the Empire Air Training Scheme, who arrived in Britain a couple of weeks ago, already have been in combat and have flown over German-held territory.

### 48 Hours After Arrival.

Pilot Officer Arthur Snell, of Ottawa, who qualified as navigator, bomb aimer, wireless operator and gunner, was the first of the new Canadian airmen to go into action and within 48 hours of his arrival in England he helped bomb Boulogne, one of the Nazi invasion bases on the French coast.

The bomber in which he was a member of the crew raced in to the target, dropping incendiary bombs, starting half a dozen fires to help illuminate the target for other British bombers, and then circled back to unload a cargo of high explosives.

Snell, who wears an observer's wing, gained his commission under the plan, after joining as an aircraftman second class at the outbreak of the war.

---

Of interest to Old Boys who have recently left the School, was the picture of R.C.N.V.R. Headquarters which appeared in the *Citizen* a short time ago, and which showed V. J. "Mony" Wilgress in the act of giving instruction in wireless telegraphy.

We congratulate, most heartily, G. C. Simonds on his promotion to the rank of Lieutenant-Colonel.

E. T. C. Orde, we are pleased to note, is now a Lieut.-Commander in the R.C.N.V.R.

And we also reproduce another press account which has just reached us:

## OTTAWA OFFICER ESCAPES BULLETS OF DISGRUNTLED GERMAN PILOT

Lieut. T. R. (Mike) Wood Tells of Exciting Experiences in Letter Home—
15 Mile Route Marches for S.D. and G. Highlanders.
(By W. Q. Ketchum.)

Being machine-gunned by a disgruntled German pilot who was coming down low to land his disabled aircraft was the experience of Lieut. T. R. (Mike) Wood, of Ottawa. He is a son of Lieut.-Colonel Edward H. Wood, 151 Metcalfe street. His brother, Arthur, formerly of Ashbury College, is a lieutenant in the 1st Battalion, Governor General's Foot Guards.

"Mike", who is serving in the 1st Corps Troops Supply Column has written to friends here of his novel experience. "I have been shot at! That's an awful way to start a letter, but there it is. Two days ago a German 'plane that had been disabled came down low to land and on his way machine-gunned everything in sight. My car was one of those things. He put three holes in the front right hand fender, but that's all—missed me and the car!

"Yesterday we had a huge dog-fight over our camp involving about 40 or 50 aircraft. In one area 14 German and one British machine were shot down—two very close. The fights started at about 18,000 feet, but before they were through they were down to about 1,500 and looking strangely like a swarm of over-sized, angry bees.

"Last night they really went to work on this area—22 bombs in all—seven un-exploded. I had the windshield of my car smashed by a piece of shrapnel, but my driver wasn't hurt."

---

Many Old Boys who left McGill recently are with the R.C.A.F.: Desmond Black is at Brandon, Manitoba, Jim Calder is at Windsor Mills, Russell Cowans is at Regina, and Don Patterson is stationed in Ottawa.

Bill Hadley is a Captain in the R.C.A. at "some eastern Canadian port." Hadley, it will be remembered, achieved distinction and prominence at the Royal Military College after he left Ashbury.

In this issue of the Ashburian, we are pleased to print an article by Lieutenant W. H. Ellis on the problems that confront the Services. Ellis, a former Editor of the Magazine, has been on Active Service with the Governor General's Foot Guards since 1939. He was on Special Duty Detachment with the regiment until June this year, when he was appointed Intelligence Officer of the first Battalion, G.G.F.G. Now, Bill is Adjutant of the Second Battalion. It will be recalled that he was married recently in the Bishop Strachan School Chapel to the former Susan Irene Cockburn of Toronto.

Trinity House, Toronto,
Dec 10, 1940.

Dear Sir,

Why pick on me for Old Boy news when there are so many abler men for the task? For instance, J. C. Phillips, right here in Trinity, would have been only too glad to take time off from his soccer to write it for you. When "J.C." is not busy pulling the Trinity soccer team into play-offs, he spends his time, among other things, in breezing through the second year of the pass Arts course.

Then there is James E. Hyndman, also in Trinity, who has successfully entered the second year of the Law course. He also takes an active part in C.O.T.C. activities. On Mondays he drills for two hours, and on Saturday afternoons plods merrily along with the rest of his platoon, up hill and carefully down dale, scheming to outwit "the enemy" in tactical exercises in High Park.

To complete this list of Trinity Ashburians, there is Ted Wilgress in the first year of the Law course in the University.

Don Snell is studying electrical engineering this year. He shines in the C.O.T.C., and was in the select Guard of Honour which was inspected by the Governor General, who received the honorary degree of LL.D. here last Friday.

Other Old Boys whom I know are here in Toronto, but have not seen yet, are: Allan S. Purdy, second year, Forestry, in the U. of T.; Bill Fullerton, who graduated from McGill and is studying Law at Osgoode Hall; and "Joe" Hobbs whom I knew in the Junior School. He is now working at Malton, but is not yet in the R.C.A.F.

John Dixon was in Trinity last year, but I can't find a trace of him this year.

Now, surely, Sir, any one of those could spout higher, as a fountain of news, than I can. I lay claim to an insignificant place in the list of those in the pass Arts course, and muddling a bit in C.O.T.C. work.

Finally, George Wodehouse is in Toronto finishing a medical course. He is an intern at the Toronto General Hospital.

I hope I haven't missed anyone. Can you (a) read this, and (b) separate the grain from the chaff? If so, I am,

Yours sincerely,

Peter Viets.

162 Earl St., Kingston, Ont.,
Dec. 10, 1940.

Dear Sir,

You doubtless ask for news of this vicinity because of the excellent showing the Queen's men made in the Old Boys' football game. Their numbers were small, but their quality—well, you saw the game!

Howie Barends is our senior representative here this year and he is working hard in medicine. In the Arts Faculty are Avery Dunning, Tom Galt and John Wallace. Ave is in his final year, and Tom is keeping up the good work he started last year when he just managed to scrape through with two scholarships.

Newcomers to the campus are Robert Wilson and Adrian Phillips. Bob is in Arts, while Ade is taking an Arts-Science course, preparatory to writing his Royal Canadian Naval exams this Spring. With the graduation of Ted Brown last year, Donald "D" is the only Science man on the campus.

Across the water at R.M.C., Bob Stedman is a Senior. He still has time, however, to carry on a violent affair. (If this is not censored I shall be killed.) Bert Lawrence and Elliot Spafford are undergoing the miseries of their recruit year, but they seem to be getting some enjoyment out of it as well.

Three Old Boys who took advantage of their C.O.T.C. course last year, are the Perley-Robertson twins and Bill Robinson, all of whom are now with the Artillery at Petawawa. Hugh "Mass" Baker is also at Petawawa with the Engineers.

It might be of interest for you to hear that Eric Earnshaw is now in His Majesty's Destroyer *Firedrake*, but expects to be sent back to the *Renown* shortly.

And now, as my index finger is nothing but a piece of raw flesh from tapping at this typewriter, I shall close without more ado.

Sincerely,

Donald Maclaren.

_____

3605 University St.,
Montreal, P. Que.,
Dec. 10, 1940.

Dear Sir,

On receiving your telegram, "I understand Green got your address wrong. Please send up McGill news overnight—the frantic Porritt," I was at first puzzled. However, as it has been my privilege to supply the Ashburian with news of its Old Boys here at McGill for the last few issues, I think I grasped its meaning, and am now equally as frantic in trying to supply you with what you asked.

While the numbers are somewhat fewer than in previous years, you will have to agree that the high quality makes up for this loss.

Ian Barclay, for example, in keeping with his "battleship" characteristics, played a star rôle with McGill's "Navy" football team this fall. I also understand he is keeping up his usually high (?) academic standard.

Mickey Crerar, besides continuing his second year engineering course, finds time to vent his spirits in critical letters about one thing and another to the university daily paper.

Bill Grant is now carrying on his work in third year Arts, and while he is not pursuing his athletic inclinations, he is becoming a very proficient homemaker, in that he is house manager of the Kapps this year.

"Bingie" McCallum, after spending a year at the university of Syracuse, has seen his way clear to come to McGill, where he is taking up engineering and engaging in various sports.

"José" McCallum, while here mainly to get a B.A., is also taking advantage of most of the university's many extra-curricular activities. I don't think he ever has a spare moment; if he isn't writing some article for the McGill Daily, you will probably find him playing English rugger, or attending some Political Science meeting.

"Chippy" Reynolds, "the Meadowmouse" to most people, is following up his studies in Commerce. He is not selling many typewriters nowadays, since his signal failure wth you. (Are you there, Snelling?)

Andy Hersey, after a short spell at L.C.C., has come here in an attempt to rescue a Bachelor of Arts degree.

Angus Wilson has remained as elusive as the Scarlet Pimpernel. From what I can find out, however, he is taking his first year pre-medical work.

Geoffrey Wright will graduate this year with a B.Sc. He, like MacCallum, has been taking part in almost every thing that comes along.

So ends the McGill news, but I have jotted down a few names of Old Boys who were here recently.

Bill Baskerville is with the Canada Can Company, and is in our C.O.T.C. Sidney Drew is at the University of British Columbia, while Jimmy Kirkpatrick is still playing golf in Vancouver. Ian Macorquodale is working with the Northern Electric Company, while his brother Fraser, is with the Law firm, Mann, LaFleur and Brown.

David Stewart is apprenticed to his father's business, Macdonald cigarettes.

I could hardly let this letter go without saying how privileged I feel that, in the School's fiftieth year, you have asked me again to tell you some of the Old Boy activities here.   It's a proud fiftieth year for Ashbury—able to take care of a complete English Prep school besides having its own members increased, and turning out such highly spirited teams as the football one, among many other things.

Hoping this will be of some interest.

Frantically yours,

Frank Burrows.

---

## AN OPEN LETTER TO THE OLD BOYS' ASSOCIATION

Dear Sir,

I must confess that the first impetus for this letter was derived from the gallant efforts of Ian Barclay and José McCallum to restore to the Association something of its "pep", and if I might use a little of the Magazine's space to offer a few suggestions as to how a closer tie between the School and the Old Boys could be achieved, I should be most grateful.

The problem which the Magazine faces each year in collecting Old Boy notes becomes, it seems, ever increasingly difficult.   It is only the work of one or two Old Boys at McGill, Queen's, and Toronto that enables us to publish any form of university notes. Your editors receive only two forms of letters: those containing cheques—very welcome—for advertisements, and letters written for the sole purpose of correcting some item of information published in the last issue.   We never mind apologizing for misinformation, or correcting statements given to us in error, but if, in the first place, information had been sent in by the Old Boy concerned, the accuracy of our reporting would be guaranteed.   This was mentioned in our last number, but obviously to no purpose.   We do not mind complaints, if the complaints are surrounded with news, but when the total number of letters received up to the deadline of this issue's going to press is exactly one, excepting the university letters asked for by the Staff, it must augur something amiss.   Surely each and every Old Boy should look upon it as his very small duty to contribute in some way to the publication of the Magazine of whose Staff in former years he himself might have been a member, or even an editor.

It does not occur to me that when I, too, am an Old Boy I shall be immune to the somewhat natural tendency to drift away from the old School, but now, while I am here, I see what the Old Boys' Association *can* do for the School, and I hope that when I leave I may be one of those privileged to change that *"can* do" to *"is* doing."

F. Barclay Robinson, your President, has appealed to you to write to him, whether to criticize or laud any feature of the Association. It is our hope that you will write to the Magazine as well.

If I have repeated myself time and again, it is with a purpose in mind. Mr. Porritt, your Editor-in-Chief as well as ours, has recently been asked to act as Liaison Officer between the Old Boys and the School. He has done fine work, I think we must all agree, in the first job, and will do, we can be sure, equally well in the new responsibility he has assumed. But without cooperation from the Old Boys themselves, the work he has to do will be impossible and the style "Liaison Officer" merely a sinecure.

Yours sincerely,

G. D. Hughson.

---

We congratulate Jack Hose on his recent engagement to Miss Edith McCrimmon of Toronto. Jack is now in command of the R.C.N.V.R. at Ottawa.

---

We regret to report the death of Mrs. Hedley Bridge, wife of a former Master at Ashbury. To her family we offer our sincere sympathy on behalf of the School.

---

Edward P. Taylor has just been appointed by the Hon. C. D. Howe as a member of the executive committee of the Department of Munitions and Supply. He is one of the leading business men of Canada who are voluntarily contributing to the war effort. We congratulate him most sincerely upon surviving, along with Mr. Howe, the recent torpedoing of the *Western Prince.*

Ted Devlin, one of the best-known announcers on the C.B.C. net-work, is still forging ahead. As may be remembered, Ted gave the commentary for the Royal Visit Broadcasts last year. He is now announcing for the C.B.C. String Orchestra and the Toronto Philharmonic, among other things.

Graham Brown has just received his Bachelor of Science degree from Queen's, and is at present working in the Canadian National Carbon Company at Toronto. He has already completed his thirty days of compulsory training.

Fraser Macorquodale, who is mentioned also in Burrow's letter, has recently broken into histrionics again, with a performance of Shaw's "The Dark Lady of the Sonnets" in Montreal, in which he was both actor and commentator.

Eric Blackburn acted as an usher at the Cartier-Coristine wedding in Ottawa recently. He is now a Lieutenant in the Princess Louise Dragoon Guards.

Don Paterson also acted as usher, at the Francis-Paterson wedding. Don is a leading aircraftsman.

---

The following is taken from the Evening *Citizen.*

### TELLING LONDON

' "A people who have beaten ten years of depression and seven years of drought," Mr. R. T. Bowman told Londoners at lunch the other day, "are not likely to be frightened at the sight of a lot of mere Nazis."

'Mr. Bowman, noted Canadian broadcaster, gave an illuminating talk on Canada's war effort—well seasoned with humor about the amateur soldiers' early blunders.

'He assessed for his listeners the Dominion's incentives to taking part in the war, the pro-British and anti-Nazi feeling, the value of the royal visit and generally the reaction of the Canadian people whom he described as "ten millions eating their hearts out to help."

'A wisecrack about Canadian airmen delighted everyone.

' "They're afraid of nothing," he said. "They've got nerves like those in a set of false teeth!"

We are proud to remember that Bob attended Ashbury from 1921 to 1928.

---

Due to the war and its call upon men, many offices in the Old Boys' Association's executive have had to be temporarily relinquished and placed in other hands. Cargill Southam is now the acting president of the Old Boys' Association, in temporary succession to W. R. Eakin, on Active Service.

With a view to strengthening the ties between the Old Boys' Association and the School, it was decided to ask a Master to act as "Liaison Officer" between the two bodies. Because of his intimate connexion with the Ashburian, which, in itself is a "Liaison Officer", your Editor-in-Chief has taken on that position.

---

*We are anxious to put up Honour Boards in the School, with a complete list of Head Prefects or School Captains, back to 1910, when the School moved to its present site. We have a list as far back as 1914-1915, but would be glad of authoritative information as to whether—*

1) *Head Prefect and School Captain were ever synonymous terms.*

2) *If so, during what years.*

3) *Who held those positions during the years 1910, 1911, 1912, and 1913.*

**CAPTAIN OF THE SCHOOL**
FORMER DOMINION BOYS' TENNIS CHAMPION

# THE PREFECTS

## C. R. Burrows, Captain of the School

CHARLIE was born in 1923 and came to Ashbury in 1936, when he entered the Senior School. Since then Charlie has interested himself in all school sports, at the same time obtaining good marks in his studies. This year he is Capt. of Football, Vice-Capt. of Hockey and Cricket and is Second-in-Command of the Cadet Corps. · He is a double colour in the former two and he won his Cricket Colours last year. A remarkable all-round athlete, Burrows has also won the Junior, Intermediate and Senior Sports' Championships, as well as the Badminton and Tennis titles. ·In this latter sport Charlie was two years ago, Boys' Dominion Champion, and the recipient of a Civic Crest from the Mayor of Ottawa. Charlie is, finally, Captain of Woollcombe House. What our School Captain intends doing after he leaves Ashbury is not yet decided, but the Air Force seems to offer certain definite attractions.

## G. D. Hughson, Captain of the Boarders.

Geoff first beamed on the World in 1924 and entered Ashbury at the age of 14, and has since taken an ever active part in all School activities, social and otherwise. Geoff was a member of last year's Cricket XI and first XII, earning his Colours this year as a member of the latter. Besides being Captain of the Boarders, Hughson is a platoon commander in the Cadet Corps and has been a holder of many form prizes. For two years Geoff has been a member of the Senior Ski team and last year he acted in "The Man in the Bowler Hat". A keen student of Foreign Affairs, he has ever been interested in promoting international good-will with, we understand, some success.

## J. A. Smart

Roaring into the West in 1921, and not liking it, he roared East in 1936 He has been roaring ever since. .His strength, which he has lent so conspicuously to the Senior Football team during the last four years, his all-round ability and his unfailing good humour, have won him a host of friends. He is a two Colour man and an N.C.O. in the Cadets. Last year he appeared with the Dramatic Society in "The Bishop's Candlesticks." Though essentially a studious chap he *has* been known to indulge in the lighter side of life and is a triple-threat man on the dance floor.

## A. M. M. Curry

"Weeping showers of senseless tears," the Navy's little blessing came into the world in 1923, and temporarily loaned Mike to us in 1934. Since then Mike has almost stopped crying, and has been a most consistent supporter of the Dramatic Society, turning in some really able performances. The amount of advertisements in this issue of the Ashburian reflect greatly on his work as Advertising Manager. Mike is Captain of Connaught House, a member of the Senior Rugby Team and a Lieutenant in the Cadet Corps. He is also a member of the Ski Team. His hobbies are two-fold—launching ships, and playful badinage.

### J. A. MacGowan

Jimmy was born with a silver skate in his mouth in 1923. Twelve years later he came to Ashbury and has been the star of all our Hockey Teams ever since. Last year he was, and this year is, Captain of the First VI. He has been a Hockey Colour for the last three years and this year was awarded his Colours in Rugby. After parading with the Corps, in which he is an N.C.O., it is said that he goes home and takes it out on the car, which he still thinks is powerful enough to take off, had it got wings. In the summer Jimmy is noted for what he does in a Sea Flea.

### G. W. Green

Flap was born in 1923, and Ashbury claimed him for her own when he was thirteen. A keen soccer player, the class-room is really his métier, and the amount of books, prizes, and so on, that he has taken home after each Closing has been fabulous. Vice-captain of Connaught House, Green's main non-schoolroom activity has been with the Cadet Corps. A Platoon Commander last year, Flap was promoted to the rank of Cadet Major and is this year the Corps Leader. We may rest assured that when the Inspection takes place it will reflect most generously on his hard work.

*J. Crabb.*

THE LECTURE ROOM

CADET CORPS INSPECTION BY REAR ADMIRAL NELLES, 1940.

# THE CADET CORPS

### Reviewed by Cadet-Major G. W. Green

WITH the war entering its second year, cadet activities have become increasingly important. Although the corps was greatly handicapped by the departure of Mr. Johnson, who had, for the past five years, given much of his time to drill and advanced instruction, we feel that in Sgt.-Major Cox, late of the Royal Canadian Dragoons, we have found a worthy successor. His enthusiasm has led us into work which we have either not attempted before, or into which we have not gone far enough. Shooting has taken a primary place in the list, and ordinary squad drill has become increasingly important. Those of the Corps who have drilled under Sgt.-Major Cox this term already show an unaccustomed snap and sparkle, which, we trust, will spread to the raw recruits.

Unfortunately, our rifles were recalled by the Department of National Defence early in the year, leaving rifle drill an unknown subject to many of the new boys. No visible distress has been observed among Cadets of three or four years standing.

The large number of new boys has made it imperative to seek out other activities in which all can indulge without swelling the squads to unmanagable size. First aid has already started among the smaller boys, for the most part those from Abinger Hill School, and it is hoped that semaphore or map reading instruction may be given to those Cadets who are far enough advanced in other branches. It had been planned to set up a course in machine-gunnery, but the number of these weapons now available for such use appears to be very small. Beyond one battered specimen of World War vintage, none have been found.

During this term, several cadets have been promoted to non-commissioned ranks. G. R. Goodwin and H. J. MacDonald were made Platoon Sergeants; and J. A. Smart, J. A. MacGowan, R. B. Bailey, G. S. Fisher, section leaders.

Our outside activities have naturally been reduced by the departure of our parent regiment, the Governor General's Foot Guards, from Ottawa. The Corps did not participate in the Armistice Day Parade as usual this year, for that reason. We hope, however, to produce a Cadet Corps on Inspection Day which will do credit both to the Regiment and the School, and which will show that every member of the Corps is fully aware of the responsibility resting upon the shoulders of those who are training in preparation for His Majesty's services.

# GAMES

FOOTBALL, 1940.

# FOOTBALL

## SEASON 1940

### By C. R. Burrows, Captain, 1940

THIS season, with only two Colours remaining from last year, but with the majority of last year's team returning, the prospects for a good season were high.

There was a larger turnout than usual and much new blood to work on.

After a few practice games the team was ready for its old rivals, Bishop's and L.C.C. We were able to defeat Bishop's with comparative ease, but lost to L.C.C. by a touchdown on the last play of the game.

In spite of the disappointment of losing the championship by such a narrow margin, the 1940 football season may be considered most satisfactory.

The team would like to thank Mr. Brain for his untiring effort and patience in coaching. It is no reflection on his good work that the school lost by so slight a margin the football championship of 1940.

## FIRST XII

J. P. THOMAS: Vice-Captain, 3rd year on team. Flying Wing. An excellent ball carrier, whose weight and speed gained many yards for us. His kicking and forward passing were good, and his spirit was invaluable to the team.

G. D. HUGHSON: 2nd year on team. Quarterback. His field generalship was faultless and he was one of the hardest working members on the team. His tackling on the secondary was excellent.

H. J. MacDONALD: 2nd year on team. Outside. One of the best outsides the school has had for a long time. Sure catch and very seldom missed a tackle. His experience will be a great asset to next year's team.

J. A. MacGOWAN: 2nd year on team. Outside. Another very fine outside, whose combination with MacDonald was hard to beat. His downfield tackling was excellent and he had a sure pair of hands.

J. A. SMART: 4th year on Team. Middle. With his excellent plunging could always be relied upon to gain us many useful yards. His interference in the line was always good, but his tackling on the defence could be improved.

G. S. FISHER: 2nd year on team. Half. Was the hardest tackler on the team, and missed very few tackles on the secondary. His plunges, although slow, were quite good.

GOODWIN: 2nd year on team. Middle. Plunged well at times, and his tackling was greatly improved over last year.

WARDROPE: 2nd year on team. Inside. His tackling on the line was good, but his interference was not what it should have been.

HEATH: 2nd year on team. Inside. Tackled hard on the secondary, but his interference on the line was weak.

WINTER: 2nd year on team. Snap. His snapping was faultless all season, and although light he made some fine tackles. His experience gained this year should be valuable to next year's team.

McKINLEY: 1st year on team. Spare Inside. His tackling on the line was good, but could improve greatly on his interference.

BRONSON: 2nd year on team. Spare Half. Fastest member of the team, but must learn how to handle the ball.

LEGGETT: 2nd year on team. Spare Inside. Tried hard. His interference was good at times, but should learn to use his weight to better advantage.    .

CROIL: 1st year on team. Spare Half. Tackled well, and with more experience should become a valuable player.

CURRY: 1st year on team. Spare inside and snap. Although handicapped by weight, showed great keeness, and made good interference.

LEE: 2nd year on team. Spare Lineman. His tackling was good but lacked experience.

CONYERS: 1st year on team. Half. Did some nice tackling in the secondary at the first of the season, but slackened off towards the end. Plunged well at times.

LAWSON: 1st year on team. Spare Quarter. Was a plucky tackler although greatly handicapped by his size. Must learn to run forward instead of across the field.

### By A. D. Brain, Esq.

C. R. BURROWS: Captain, 3rd year on team. Half. A fine all-round backfielder, where plunging, end-running and forward passing were invaluably effective, his running back of kicks from the safety position also gained much valuable distance. As Captain, he inspired and maintained great keenness, and handled his team well, both on and off the field.

## THE MATCHES

### VERSUS U. of O. SENIORS, LOST 5 - 17

We opened our season with an exhibition game against Ottawa University at Varsity Oval. Getting off to a shaky start we were behind on the scoring column by a converted touchdown before the first quarter ended. Smart plunged over in the second quarter for what proved to be our only score of the game, but the convert was missed and we were still behind by the count of 6 - 5. Our opponents gathered eleven more points in the last half and the final whistle found us on the short side of a 17 - 5 score. The team seemed over-eager individually and hence did not function well as a unit.

## VERSUS NEPEAN SENIORS, LOST 13 - 18

The second game of the season was another exhibition, played at Ashbury, the annual encounter with Nepean High School.

Benefitting from the experience gained in the first game, the School put up a very good game and only accepted defeat after a hard fight. We opened the scoring early in the game, but were inclined to loosen a little until Nepean went into the lead. Every point after that was well earned. Thomas kicked a field goal, tying the game at 13 - 13, in the third quarter, but an aerial attack in the last stanza proved too much for us and Nepean won by virtue of their last touchdown 18 - 13.

## VERSUS NEPEAN SENIORS, LOST 5 - 13

On the third game of the year the Ashbury team clashed with Nepean Seniors for the second consecutive encounter, but this time we were determined to conquor them.

However, the confidence was not entirely justified, for in the first quarter Nepean broke away, scoring a touch and converting it.

Hopes were raised in the second quarter, however, when Thomas intercepted a Nepean forward pass on their thirty yard line and ran it back for Ashbury's five points. Burrows' attempted convert was blocked.

At the beginning of the second half the score was 6 - 5 in favour of Nepean. This half proved disastrous to the school team, for with Nepean's kick from our twenty-five yard line Burrows was rouged, giving them another point. This was followed by a touchdown which was unconverted, making the final score 13 - 5 in favour of Nepean.

## VERSUS ST. PATRICK'S COLLEGE, WON, 38 - 6.

On Saturday, October 19, Ashbury played host to the unbeaten St. Patrick's College Junior team in an exhibition match. The visitors were without the services of two of their best players, but as the game proceeded, senior replacements joined their ranks, and the play was well contested. Both teams took advantage of every break, but St. Pat's only reward was when they fell on the ball behind our line after a kick had been fumbled. The School had an edge in the play throughout and showed none of that easing off tendency that had appeared in previous games when we were ahead on the scoring column.

THE ANNEXE

## VERSUS BISHOP'S COLLEGE SCHOOL, AWAY, WON 17 - 11

Our annual encounter with B.C.S. was played in Montreal on Saturday, October 26. The field was muddy, the day dull, and a slight wind blew across the length of the field.

Bishop's kicked off and the ball was run back to the thirty yard line where it was first down for Ashbury. Two plays later Thomas ran around left end to start an extension play with Burrows, and ran sixty yards for the only major score of the first half. The convert was missed, and both teams began the grim battle of trying to gain ground, going one way and then the other, as one was momentarily superior. Our opponents presented a heavier side, outweighing us in every department, and before half time there were several casualties. Hughson was injured so badly in making a tackle that he had to be taken to hospital.

The third quarter began with Ashbury leading by the score of 5 - 0, but Bishop's started with a steam roller attack which ended in a touchdown soon after the second half was under way. They converted and momentarily rested on a 6 - 5 lead. The School, however, moved into Bishop's territory and after missing a field goal, Thomas went over for another major score which Burrows converted. B.S.C. retaliated and in the last moments of the third quarter they tied the score at 11 - 11.

It remained unchanged until late in the final stanza, when MacDonald received a forward pass for a sensational thirty yard gain which gave Ashbury a first down on Bishop's ten yard stripe. Then Burrows called for a kick formation, thus drawing the opposing team's defence into a closely packed bunch, and then instead of kicking he skirted the end on a ten yard touchdown run. Thomas converted from placement. Bishop's pushed hard, but gained little ground, and the final whistle found Ashbury the victor by a 17 - 11 margin.

Chief casualty to our team, besides Hughson, was Goodwin, with a broken collar bone.

## VERSUS LOWER CANADA COLLEGE, LOST 8 - 12

On Saturday, November 2nd, the Lower Canada College team came to Ashbury to play for the championship. Both teams had previously beaten B.C.S. and the winner of today's match would hold football supremacy in the triangular circuit.

Ashbury kicked off, and the visiting team brought the ball into our territory before being forced to kick. We failed to make any gain on the first two downs and the team went into kick formation. Something went wrong, however; L.C.C. swarmed in before Burrows could get the kick away, and a touchdown was the result. Lower Canada converted, then kicked off to Ashbury.

The first play was an extension to the right, Burrows to Thomas, in which the latter carried the ball eighty yards for a major score. The convert was missed and

H. D. L. SNELLING

L.C.C. received the kick off. Each team collected a single before half time and when the third quarter got under way Lower Canada lead by a point, the score being 7 - 6.

The third quarter saw both teams pushing hard with Ashbury reaping full scoring honours. Late in the quarter Burrows attempted a field goal. It went wide, but was good for one point and the game was at a deadlock, remaining so until very late in the final quarter.

Thomas received a kick behind his own goal line and just managed to get out of the end zone before being tackled. Then from a first down on the one yard line the School displayed a spectacular march, and when it was finally stopped Burrows dropped back and kicked. Conyers made the tackle for the rouge which put us ahead 8 - 7.

Then L.C.C. opened up with a wide-open attack. Several penalties against Ashbury aided them also and on the final play of the game they plunged over for a touchdown to be victorious by the score of 12 - 8.

## VERSUS LISGAR COLLEGIATE, LOST 13 - 18

In an exhibition game, a Lisgar Collegiate team composed of senior and junior players, defeated the School 18 - 13.

Trailing by 7 - 6 going into the last quarter, Lisgar shoved across two touchdowns, both being converted. Ashbury came back hard and in the last two minutes of the game Thomas plunged for a touchdown which was converted. It was, however, too late for Ashbury to score the winning points and when the final whistle went, Lisgar was ahead 18 - 13. MacDonald scored the first touchdown on a pass from Thomas, who also kicked the other points.

The Ashbury line up for the games was as follows: Flying wing, Thomas; halves, Burrows, Fisher and Conyers; quarter, Hughson; snap, Winter; insides, Heath and Wardrope; middles, Smart and Goodwin; outsides, MacDonald and MacGowan; subs, Andrews, Croil, Curry, Lee, Lawson, Leggett, and McKinley.

## VERSUS OLD BOYS, LOST, 5 - 8
### By H. D. L. Snelling, Esq.

First of all I should like to say that we the Old Boys won eight to five. I can't believe it either yet, but it's true, because none of our friends have remarked that they saw by the papers that we played our usual game, or that they heard that we had taken our usual beating. They just seem a bit superior; they don't want to discuss it at all; they don't want any part of it.

After writing up the Ashbury Old Boys' account, man and boy, for some years, and always writing as a member of the losing side, you can realize my feelings in describing a match that the Old Boys won, and trying to give a bogus impression of studied impartiality. An Old Boy just can't do that sort of thing.

I believe it is customary to give the line-up. We were a cosmopolitan lot, seventeen strong, approved of and obviously admired by two stray dogs. They howled very well over some of the more doubtful decisions, as we all did too, but I'll wager that they knew more while they were howling than we did. The School were all dressed alike. Somebody kept demanding that I take his boots off—he seemed to think that I had pinched them—but he was too innocent to realize that I also had his pants and his headgear. And now for the account.

We were blessed—*I* was cursed—with advantage in weight, and therefore we plunged most of the time. Very early in the game, after spectacular, not to say brilliant play, one of our drawbacks scampered down the sideline for a touchdown. A very creditable feat indeed, which we converted to lead six-nothing. Taking advantage of our "jubilation" (it sounds better than "condition") Joe Thomas, when we were all looking the other way, ran through our side for a major score. Completely outclassed in converting, their attempt on this occasion was silly, and the half ended 6 - 5 in our favour.

Now here was the rub. We were quite content to shake hands and leave, but youth took advantage of us men and they wouldn't have it.

After half time everyone thought the last half would be a riot for the school. So did we. It wasn't, though, for we scored two more points on a safety touch, when one of our linemen tripped through and couldn't get out of the way of the ball-carrier.

We would like to say in conclusion that we all enjoyed the game to the utmost. No one was hurt but our most ardent spectator, one of the stray dogs, and the feelings of those to whom the second half of the game was living torture.

# SOCCER

## THE SEASON
### Reviewed by R. T. Holmes
#### FIRST XI

OWING to the influx of soccer players from England and elsewhere there has been a considerable increase in our numbers this year. We have had two games against Lower Canada College, and we had hopes of playing Trinity College School, but this project unfortunately fell through.

As most of the team will be here next year, there are good prospects for another successful season.

## THE MATCHES

### VERSUS LOWER CANADA COLLEGE, WON 1 - 0

On October 26th, the Lower Canada College Soccer XI played the School on the home grounds. There was a strong wind blowing straight down the field, and Ashbury played against it during the first half.

Due, mainly, to the difficulty of taking the ball against the wind, the play was mostly in the Ashbury half, but no goal was scored. There was an exciting moment when L.C.C. succeeded in getting the ball through the goal off a corner, but fortunately, this was ruled off-side.

At half time there was no score, and the second half saw a constant and intensive attack by the School forwards. However, every attempt seemed to go wrong at the last minute, until, eventually, McLaren I succeeded in getting the ball past the enemy's goal-keeper.

This was the first and last score of the game.

The line-up was as follows: Goal, Montgomery; Backs, Bourget, Nairn; Half Backs, Ney, Holmes I, Lawrence; Forwards, Viets, Mordy, McLaren I, Woodward I, Bailey.

### VERSUS LOWER CANADA COLLEGE, DRAW, 1 - 1

On Friday, November 1st, the Senior Soccer XI concluded their season by playing Lower Canada College in Montreal.

The game began, as in the home match, by Ashbury playing uphill. The L.C.C. forward and half back lines kept the School defence busy by hammering at the Ashbury goal during the first half, varied by occasional break-aways by the School forwards.

However, there was no score at half-time, and Ashbury took the other end, full of hope.

The second half was more even, the ball flew from one end of the field to the other, and then back again. The play was, however, slightly in Ashbury's favour, when L.C.C. managed to score a goal. But the School piqued by this catastrophe, were not long in avenging the loss. McLaren I succeeded in scoring, five minutes later. When the whistle blew, not long after, the score was 1 - 1.

The line-up was as follows: Goal, Sablin; Backs, Bourget, Nairn; Half Backs, Ney, Holmes I, Green I; Forwards, Viets, Mordy, McLaren I, Woodward I, Bailey.

## THE HOUSE MATCHES

The first of the annual series of soccer games between Connaught House and Woollcombe House took place on Tuesday, November 19th.

The ground was mostly covered with snow, which made it very slippery, and was responsible for many of the faults on both sides.

Connaught was playing on the offensive, and before half-time, they scored with an excellent shot by Viets. Woollcombe was faced, at half-time, not only with the difficulty of keeping Connaught away from their goal, but also of scoring once to equalize or twice to win.

Actually, the only other score was for Woollcombe by MacGowan, and the match was drawn 1 - 1.

Connaught House: Goal, Montgomery; Backs, Nairn, Leggett; Half Backs, Fisher, Lawrence, MacDonald I; Forwards, Viets, Thomas I, McLaren I, Heath, Bulpit.

Woollcombe House: Goal, Goodwin; Backs, Smart, Bourget; Half Backs, Hughson II; Holmes I, Conyers; Forwards, Mordy, Bronson, Woodward I, MacGowan, Bailey.

The conflict was continued on the following day, November 20th. By this time the snow had practically disappeared, and both sides were playing better.

Although it was Woollcombe this time who dominated the game, there was no goal by half-time. In the second half, Connaught pressed, but they were frustrated in every likely attempt at a goal. The Woollcombe forwards made one spectacular break-away, when Woodward I almost scored, but the ball went over, instead of into, the goal.

There was no score at all in this game, and so the series was drawn.

Woollcombe House: Goal, Goodwin; Backs, Smart, Bourget; Half Backs, Croil, Holmes I, Hughson II; Forwards, Wardrope, Mordy, Woodward I, MacGowan, Bronson.

Connaught House: Goal, Montgomery; Backs, Lee, MacDonald I; Half Backs, Fisher, Lawrence, Green I; Forwards, Viets, Thomas I, McLaren I, Heath, Bulpit.

Bailey Captained the Senior XI, and Green I was vice-captain.

## UNDER 15

### VERSUS LOWER CANADA COLLEGE, WON, 4 - 3

It was a very fine day with a little wind. Ashbury won the toss and kicked off. After ten minutes, Ashbury scored a goal, but within five minutes L.C.C. had scored one also. Before the end of the first half, Ashbury scored two more and, at half-time, the score was 3 - 1.

In the first five minutes of the second half, Ashbury scored another goal. After a quarter of an hour, L.C.C. scored two goals, and at the end of the game, the score was 4 - 3 for Ashbury. The playing was good on both sides.

The Ashbury scorers were Abbott-Smith, Pearson, Macnabb I and Eliot. I.

The line-up was as follows: Goal, Hurtley; Backs, Harben I, Goodeve; Half Backs, Thomas II, Pilgrim, Macnabb II; Forwards, Abbott-Smith, Pearson, Macnabb I, Thomson, Eliot I.

## VERSUS SELWYN HOUSE, LOST 0 - 3

It was a rainy day in Montreal, and as a result L.C.C. grounds, on which we played were very slippery. Selwyn House won the toss and kicked off. After some very good play on both sides, Selwyn House forced a goal. Just before the end of the first half, Hurtley kicked a goal, on which, after an unfortunate penalty, they scored a second goal.

There was a very short half-time as it was still raining.

Ashbury kicked off, but very soon another goal was scored. Selwyn House scored no more goals after this, but at times it looked as if they would. After half-time the heavy Selwyn House team seemed to affect the lighter Ashbury side  The Ashbury stars were Harben I, Macnabb II, and Pearson.

The line-up was as follows: Goal, Hurtley; Backs, Harben I, Goodeve; Half Backs, Thomas II, Pilgrim, Macnabb II; Forwards, Abbott-Smith, Pearson, Macnabb I, Thomson, Eliot I.

## VERSUS SELWYN HOUSE, WON, 4 - 0

Played on hard ground and in a fair wind the return match against Selwyn House was a better game—apart from the score—than when we played in Montreal.

The visitors kicked off but we scored early when Lawrence fooled their goal-keeper on a free-kick. For a time the ball went from end to end, but for the most part the play was in their half of the field. Before half-time Eliot I scored a second goal for the School. In the second half the wind was in our favour and the play was consequently even more in Selwyn House territory. Before the final whistle both Pearson and Thomson added goals to make the final score 4 - 0 for Ashbury.

The line up was as follows: Goal, Montgomery; Backs, Harben I, Pilgrim; Half Backs, Shaw, Lawrence, Macnabb II; Forwards, Abbott-Smith, Pearson, Prance, Thomson, Eliot I.

## COLOURS

The following have been awarded their Colours since the last issue of the Ashburian:

First XII

    J. P. Thomas

    G. D. Hughson

    H. J. MacDonald

    J. A. MacGowan

    J. A. Smart

    G. S. Fisher

First XI

    R. T. Holmes

House

| *Connaught* | *Woollcombe* |
|---|---|
| G. W. Green | G. R. Goodwin |
| J. T. H. Leggett | C. W. Woodward |
| | R. T. Holmes |

## HOCKEY

ALTHOUGH the Senior Team has not played any games up to the time of going to press, with the whole of last year's team back we hope, with practice, to regain for Ashbury the Old Boys' Cup. We hope also, to play more than our usual two inter-school games, and it is possible that one will be arranged with Trinity College School, Port Hope. It will be recalled that we owe them a visit as they played us at the Auditorium two years ago.

With the large influx of new boys, we expect this year to have three main Hockey teams, and matches will be arranged for them during the Christmas holidays.

*J. Crabb.*

## "HONI SOIT QUI MAL Y PENSE"

But they say—and they seem to know:

That a certain disciple of the wide open spaces has finally reached that hitherto unattainable state in which he wondered whether he should go home for Christmas.

That Mr. Porritt met Sir Cedric Hardwicke at the School gates. As a magnificent gesture to a fellow actor, he held out his hand. Sir Cedric's hat, according to Mr. Porritt, is a black Hamburg, and the coat which Sir Cedric threw over his arm was brown.

That Harry Green is not as yet engaged to be married, nor is Moffatt definitely best man.

That Pilgrim is "cute".

That Geoff Hughson, not as yet a fugitive from Canadian justice, is thinking of ways and means of crossing the border and seems to be contemplating a Capital to Capital trip.

That simply EVERYONE knows about Mr. Polk.

That Cadet Major G. W. Green has demanded numerous changes in K.R. & O.

That although Pilgrim blushingly enjoyed being called "cute", Mike Curry wishes that when people allude to himself, they would, with awe in every whisper, say something like "handsome brute" instead. After all, although we have seen no topless towers in flames, he did lend that face to the launching.

That the School is looking forward with great interest to the time when its senior "Navy Man" will command a "Diesel Super-Submarine"—whatever that is

They congratulate Oliver M. (Joe—"I am an American") Read III on not having been in a foreign jail since Hallowe'en.

And they also say:

That Conyers is following in the MacGowan-Viets-Bronson footsteps—and how!

That with the approach of spring just around a wintry corner, Henry Birks and Sons will once more do a rush business in School pins.

That if Mr. Sykes (Toe-hold Dick) and Mr. Harrison (Any-Hold's-Good-Enough-for-Jim) MUST stage an all-in wrestling bout, MUST they do it in the Masters' Common Room, and MUST it always be at midnight?

---

It is said that the following conversation was overheard in MacGowan's car lately as that distinguished gentleman burned up the road to the lake—

Jimmy: (full of the exhilarating autumn air) "Gosh!! It's great to be alive."

Gus (Dimple) Smart: (with an eye on the road) "Great? It's miraculous."

Phone calls are going formal this winter. When you ring up one house The Voice at the other end invariably replies, "Oliver Middleton Read III at this end."

And we hear that the Count has taken up Chinese Checkers.

And what of Bill (Orville Burke) Lawson? Where HAVE you been lately?

"Scoop" (Cab Calloway) Wait has given up photography for Terpsichore and Swing.

Roy (Playboy) Peirce has suddenly taken a keen interest in Old Boys, etc. A strange case of l'amour. That's what Shakespeare does to you, Roy!

And the tragedy is, nobody can pin anything on Fisher—much!

We understand that Mr. Brain "is the guy what's got the money," according to Makovski.

And have you heard about the Hunter versus Hunter Bowling matches? If Mrs. Hunter beats her husband (in bowling, we mean) the Juniors have a delightful morning. "Fred" lies low. Reverse the picture and you will have to imagine what the luckless Juniors go through.

We congratulate "Flap" Green on receiving his Solar Scout Wings—presented by Buck Rogers.

That distinguished military figure, Lance-Sergeant Mordy was recently heard in the quad instructing the Corps: "Squad—Whoa!"

We understand Conyers is under the impression that the result of the Battle of Taranto is Rough Riders 8, Argos 1.

Not content with his excellent showing as The Man Who Ran the National Registration, Teddy Leggett now aspires to be The Man Who Runs Our Sunday School. The mutual benefit derived supports our contention that the Crusher's motto will be, in future, Eric Knight's "Never Come Monday."

That in case by the time you have unsheathed the trusty cutlass, Geoff Hughson—in the Prefects' Common Room with the key turned—would let it be known, if it has not already been guessed, that he did not write *all* of this.

# LIBRARY NOTES

O WING to the School's increased numbers this year, several changes have been made in the library system. All reference books, have been placed in the former Junior library, while the Senior room has been entirely given over to fiction. Boys of both Schools are now able to use either library, as it was felt that those of serious mind should be given relief from the congestion around the papers and magazines.

In addition to this , the practice of signing for books has been discontinued, as a result of the increased amount of reading. It is noticable, we regret to say, that the boys from England read far more than our own do, but a certain degree of competition seems to have been introduced by this fact—exclusive of the fanatical perusal of the morning and evening papers.

We have received a gratifyingly large amount of books this term, including those from the Carnegie International Relations Club Our thanks are due to this organization for many favours, the greatest being the up-to-the-minute educational value of its publications. Among the books which we have received from them recently are: The Way Out of War; Commonwealth or Anarchy?; What Germany Forgot; Great Britain—an Empire in Transition; and American Policy in the Far East.

THE LIBRARY

# EXCHANGES

The Editors gratefully acknowledge the receipt of the following Exchanges:—

*The Acta Ridlieana*, Ridley College, St. Catherines, Ont.

*The B.C.S. Magazine*, Bishop's College School, Lennoxville, P.Q.

*The Bedales Chronicle*, Bedales School, Petersfield, Hants., England.

*The Blue and White*, Rothesay Collegiate, Rothesay, N.B.

*The Canberran*, Canberra Grammar School, Canberra, Australia.

*The College Times*, Upper Canada College, Toronto, Ont.

*The Cranbrookian*, Cranbrook School, Cranbrook, Kent, England.

*The Cranleighan*, Cranleigh School, Cranleigh, Surrey, England.

*The Felstedian*, Felsted School, Felsted, Essex, England.

*The Grove Chronicle*, Lakefield Preparatory School, Lakefield, Ont.

*The Hatfield Hall Magazine*, Hatfield Hall, Cobourg, Ont.

*The Lawrentian*, St. Lawrence College, Ramsgate, England.

*Lux Glebana*, Glebe Collegiate, Ottawa, Ont.

*The Marlburian*, Marlborough College, Marlborough, Wilts., England.

*The Meteor*, Rugby School, Rugby, England.

*The Mitre*, Bishop's University, Lennoxville, P.Q.

*Northland Echoes*, North Bay Collegiate, North Bay, Ont.

*The Patrician Herald*, St. Patrick's College, Ottawa.

*The Queen's Review*, Queen's University, Kingston, Ont.

*The Record*, Trinity College School, Port Hope, Ont.

*The R.M.C. Review*, R.M.C., Kingston, Ont.

*St. Andrew's College Review*, St. Andrew's College, Aurora, Ont.

*St. Thomas' College Magazine*, St. Thomas' College, Colombo, Ceylon

*Samara*, Elmwood School, Ottawa, Ont.

*The Shawnigan Lake School Magazine*, Shawnigan Lake, B.C.

*South African College Magazine*, S. A. High School, Cape Town

*The Tonbridgian*, Tonbridge School, Tonbridge, Kent, England.

*Trafalgar Echoes*, Trafalgar Institute, Montreal, P.Q.

*Toc H Journal*, Toc. H., Westminster, S.W.1., England.

*Toc H Chronicle*, Toc H., Westminster, S.W.1, England.

*The Trinity College Magazine*, Trinity College, Toronto, Ont.

*The Trinity Review*, Trinity University, Toronto, Ont.

*The Wanganui Collegian*, Wanganui College, Wanganui, New Zealand.

ASHBURY HOUSE

# LITERARY SECTION

# INVASION

## By G. W. Green, Editor of The Ashburian

THE rough cobblestones glimmered moistly in the dim light of the lamps as the last company turned off from the street and marched into the warehouse, heavy boots sending echoes crashing from one wooden wall to another. Kurt was faintly relieved. It had been a dreadful ordeal for him, being quartered in this old waterfront city, peopled by sullen men and silent women who crept along the pavement, their eyes tense with hatred and despair, men and women who watched the soldiers as they passed but who saw nothing, whose lips moved on the street but who spoke no word. God knows, he had tried to be friendly, but it was hard. An old woman, wrinkled and worn like his own mother, had dropped a loaf, only the other day, in the middle of the market place. He had stooped hurriedly to help her— but her eyes stopped him. Appalled by the hate he saw there he fell back, while she spat and trudged off, her bread held tightly under her arm. The Leader had said, "The people of France are now our friends", but these defeated people were not friendly they were angry and malevolent, like chained tigers. No woman had ever looked at him like that before, and it both worried and frightened him. It was good to be getting away from such things and to think once more of bringing England to her knees.

The column of men moved slowly forward, the harsh commands of the officers losing themselves in the thunderous confusion of echoes. Through the gates ahead could be seen the open sea, and a great mass of barges, rising and falling, up and down, straining at their cables and bumping together noisily. Rifles clashed to the stone floor as the long line halted. Then a second order sounded and file after file of men began to disappear out the door and vanish into the mist. The night grew colder as the outside barges moved across Kurt's vision, heading out into the Channel, leaving behind only a thin white wake.

"Number one platoon, D Company, number fourteen barge." There was a brief scramble up in the leading files, then he once more found himself moving, eyes glued religiously to the swaying pack of the man in front. As they reached the gate and turned left along the pier, a keen icy wind struck them and the files huddled closer together. There was their barge, number fourteen, a thin single-motored affair, swinging against the stone. She looked treacherous and insecure but this was no time to think of that. Down they clambered, and finding themselves seats, leaned back against their packs and braced their heavy rifles between their knees. The fog covered the sea like a grey shroud. Even the warehouse seemed a misty phantom, peopled by bodiless spirits, whose voices, in tones of command and interrogation, muttered monotonously in the darkness. Noises he would never have noticed in ordinary circumstances came to him distinctly above the slap of waves against the side and the sounds of men settling themselves in their places.

Then, as the motor, without warning, roared into life, the lantern in the bow flickered and went out. Kurt felt the boat swing around, and as she gathered way, a cold breeze whipped past, clouding his eyes and turning his breath to gusts of steam.

They were off, off to England, to free Europe forever from the harsh chains of the democracies, and to bring relief to the poor nations of the world by forcing the degenerate British to yield to the power of a young and virile Germany. Yet--what a night to save Europe! Fog so thick that the steersman was but an outline, and the water—above all, the water—greedy black waves, splashing high against the side and flowing out behind in chill oiliness, gurgling up around the boat in devilish anticipation. The very horror of it puzzled Kurt. There could be no bottom or end to it. It seemed so impersonal, cold liquid death stretching out from the coast of France to nowhere. Surely no one lived beyond this sea, struggling for life in some chill land in the midst of the waves. No, land was gone forever. They would go on and on to the edge of the world, haunted by the lapping water. He looked about him at the huddled figures of his comrades, wrapped motionless in the icy fog. Their eyes stared dully, their mouths were clamped shut. Nobody moved. Nobody spoke. God, he might have been sailing with dead men. Perhaps he was, in this unreal sea. Could he be the only human on a journey to a nameless afterworld somewhere out in the waves; he, one lone soldier of the Reich among the dead, men with no nationality? He almost laughed hysterically at the foolishness of the thought. Yet, the illusion bothered him. In an effort to shake it off he stood bolt upright and the butt of his rifle bumped noisily over the steel deck. The grey shapes stirred at last, but the sergeant's voice shouted angrily from the bow, "Quiet, there!" The light died out of his eyes and he sat down again. The sea was nothing. It had always been like that. Weren't his companions there beside him? Frantz, who had grown up with him, he certainly was not dead, for he was blowing doggedly into his cupped hands and banging his heels together in a vain attempt to restore circulation.

Yes, Frantz was indeed there. They had both been brought up together in the tradition of old Germany, the Germany of the Black Forest, Nüremburg, music boxes and the legend of the Rhine. Kurt's father had died in 1915 but he was then too young to feel the loss. His mother had taught him and advised him instead throughout his school life. She was a gentle woman, full of quiet wisdom and understanding. She had hated to see this second war come. "It is a bad thing, Kurt," she had said, "but you must do your duty to your country or life will be hard for both of us." So he had gone, feeling strangely ill at ease among the shouting ranks of young men who had paraded into camp that day in October. They were all so harsh, so fanatical. They sang loudly, songs like the "Horst Wessel" and "We are Sailing Against England." They frantically saluted every officer in sight and in the evenings ranged through the streets, laughing and boasting. Kurt could never bring himself to join them, but stayed in barracks and read what books he was allowed. As a result, he was generally looked upon with suspicion, even by Frantz. Yes, that was the hard part of it; Frantz, too, had changed. Even now, cold and miserable as they were, the boatload of men looked tense and determined. They were carrying— with characteristic thoroughness—everything necessary—and there was no glimmei of humour on any face. They just sat, keyed up to fighting pitch, and patriotically silent. Lord, they were almost hateful. He remembered the English pilot who had been shot down over Boulogne. The young fellow, prisoner though he was, had grinned regularly when the sergeant saluted. True, the Herr Sergeant's salute was something to behold, for his outstretched arm almost jerked him off his feet in its energy and his chin wobbled with enthusiasm. The last he had seen of the youngster was a jaunty figure marching off between two grim guards, whistling, to the impotent fury of those around him, the opening bars of "Deutchland Uber Alles."

It would have been fun to have been his friend. Ever since Frantz had broken away from boyish amusements, Kurt had longed for someone with whom to hunt and fish, someone like this English lad, gay and irresponsible. Every thought that he had stored up during his long loneliness he could bring into the open, and could be confided in in return. A small sound suddenly jerked him back into the present and he looked guiltily around. If the officers could have read his thoughts, what would they have said about his longing for the society of an Englishman and his contempt for his own countrymen? He shuddered and trying to check his imagination, looked around him. No one had moved. Every face bore the same tense expression. A man in the stern was methodically wiping his rifle and squinting down the barrel with gloomy satisfaction at the thought of its potential victims.

Wearied, Kurt turned around again. The cold sea still splashed about the barge, but the fog had disappeared, leaving the moon faintly visible behind the clouds. Over towards the east, the main fleet might even now be landing men below Dover. Far inland the Luftwafte was smashing great holes in the British defences, sending shrieking hell down on the poorly-equipped troops. And boys like that English prisoner were probably even now climbing into the sky, the same note of gay defiance on their lips. He could still hear that song, as clearly as if it were Frantz. It no longer sounded like the slow anthem of Germany. It seemed strangely different and —

The motors had stopped, and the barges were drifting through the slapping sea, leaving a great void of silence behind. Kurt, roused from his thoughts, watched as the officer in the bow silently stood up and slung his equipment over his shoulders. Man by man they rose, and holding their rifles high, braced themselves on the slippery deck. Still they drifted, in towards the dark shore which suddenly seemed to leap at them out of the moonlit blackness. There was no sound but that of the waves. Kurt's eyes ached as he stared tensely at the tall cliffs. In the darkness that rugged shore looked as it must have when it was still Albion, the mysterious island whose tribes waged cruel war and worshipped strange gods. The threatening rocks which had seen so many bloody struggles might even now hide men, lying in wait, their bodies pressed flat on the ground and the smell of wet grass in their nostrils. Keen eyes might be watching as men crept stealthily forward, getting into position to pour death upon the great barges as they slowly took shape in the moonlight, drifting silently in from the grey sea. The suspense was unbearable    The knowledge that . . . . .

Rrrooomm! —a sound of which he had been half conscious for several minutes broke in a deafening roar above his head. A great shadow swooped low over the barge, blotting out the white upturned faces of the soldiers. A signal lamp flickered briefly. Then, across the moon, they appeared, a tiny cloud of wide-winged bombers slowly dropping out of the sky, their motors roaring in angry triumph.

"Great God, get that motor going! Break away from the crowd!"

Men surged over the deck as they tried to reach safety. Rocked by the turmoil of their heavy feet the barge wallowed in a great trough, throwing the steersman off balance, and placing the whole boat in indescribable confusion. It was no use. A tall fountain of water shot up behind their stern and the shriek of rending metal told of the death of at least one of the fleet. Quick flashes from the cliffs answered the cries of its crew.

Then—it happened. Under his feet the deck lifted and the heaving water crashed over the side. The bow seemed to tip crazily and as it fell again into the sea, a huge five-pointed star flashed out of the smoke and Kurt fell. There was a moment of blankness; then, following his shattered rifle, his body hit the deck and he knew no more.

High up in the clouds, a bomber circling over the wreckage-strewn sea turned towards home. The young pilot did a victory role, and whistled happily as the chalk cliffs fell behind.

# "TO THE FINISH"
## By W. B. Lawson

CANADA is the home of youth. We see our destiny afar off, and the conscious-
ness that our morning hours are only dawning makes our duty clear to us.
The world needs us and this great ordeal in Europe is to be our arena.

What is the sentiment that animates us? A faith that the British name and
British institutions are worth making sacrifices for. Our sixty thousand kept that
faith, in the first great war, on the red fields of Vimy and Cambrai; they kept it above
the clouds, where many died to make the Canadian name live. Therefore, if we
would be true to those who were true to us, honour binds us to keep our contract.

Our flag symbolizes a wonderful past, and the chief glory of that past is the
memory of ancestors who have willingly died for the cause of human freedom.

Now there is laid upon us a definite obligation, "To Fight to the Finish," and
to make this dear land, which men have died to save, the hope and the blessing of
the World. We cannot live where men are treated as anything less than men.

---

# THE COUNTRY DOCTOR
## By G. W. Green

*(Parodying the literary style of all those retired medicos who court the Muse).*

FOR as long as I can remember, life has been a busy one for me, and though I
should like to spend my old age in peace and quiet, a certain belief of mine
prevents me. I believe that the lives of those who have been successful in their
profession should be made public to the world, to serve as a model and a guide to
those who would follow. To the stories of many of my fellow practitioners, therefore, I would like to add the tale of my own life, a life which has in no small way
contributed to the history of medicine.

I was born, naturally enough, in a small middle-class town in Nebraska Though
the youngest child, I was far more precocious than my brothers and sisters. Indeed,
I can still remember my grandmother shouting for hot water as I emerged into the
world, and the flurry that accompanied my christening. My childhood, however,
was normal I was greatly given to dissecting our barn cats and to vain attempts
to scalp my little playmates, but differed in no further way from the other children.
Nevertheless, my grandmother was convinced that I was worthless, and as such,

advised me to become a doctor, like my father.  My inclinations already lying in that direction, I followed my father about faithfully, holding the basin during operations, and the shaving mug when he attended in his capacity of "Tonsorial Artiste."

He was, I admit, a bit of a stranger to me.  Tall and grey, he stood out as an impressive figure in my life, and his mutton-chop whiskers, in which he so often used to hide his stethoscope, occurred again and again in my dreams.  He had been born and bred a Baptist, but his natural aversion to water had led to his expulsion from this church, and he ended his life a man of indeterminate religion.  The only other doctor in town, by reason of his cabalistic prescriptions, had been shot as a Fenian, leaving Father without a rival; an outstanding character throughout the countryside.

I can still see the old mare sleeping between the shafts, and my father clattering out of the house at midnight on an emergency call, leaving the front door wide open.  It was my job to follow him with his instrument bag, an item which he invariably forgot.

It was not until I was sixteen, I believe, that I fully understood the old man.  My mother having ventured to criticize him for some trifling fault, he calmly picked up the hatchet and knocked her to the floor.  I can never forget the noble expression of patience and humility on his fine old face as he stood over her.  He seemed to me at that moment to be god-like.  Then calling me to his side, he said,—what a deep rich voice he seemed to have—"My son, always remember the lesson I have showed you today, and you will have trouble with no one."  With these words he picked me up by the neck and threw me out into the world.

My career had begun.  I waited up the road until dark, and returning, stole Father's instrument bag and the family savings.  With the latter I purchased a moderately priced little house up-country, and gaily hung out my shingle.  Soon by dint of giving away subscriptions with each major call, I gathered together a very respectable clientele.  The work, of course, was hard, but I was never the one to balk at that.  My most frightening experience I clearly remember.  It occurred one dark wintry night as I was coming home.  The buggy had just touched the old covered bridge when my mare stopped dead and snorted angrily.  I tried to whip her on but she refused to move.  Suddenly I realized that the raging wind must have torn away the centre of the structure and that if I had gone on I should have crashed to the ice below.  I dismounted, my heart in my mouth at my narrow escape, and patting the mare gratefully, I walked forward.  Immediately there was a clatter of hoofs, and mare and buggy streaked past over the unbroken bridge into the night.  I walked home.  A great many people pretend to find horse flesh delicious.  I tried it myself but found it too coarse for good eating.

For the first few years, the petty calls of a country doctor seemed never-ending.  Conditions were terribly difficult.  My father had taught me to work by kerosene lamp, though every house in the country was wired for electricity. As a result, I was forced to have the kitchen table moved into the henhouse, where I was able to work naturally and grew to know intimately every Leghorn for twenty miles.

Time went on and brought with it new trials, new conquests. My position was established by now and I was known and beloved by young and old. Finally, one July, the great test of my teachings was thrust upon me. One of my neighbours, being in great pain, had summoned a specialist from the city. This man, however, did not succeed in helping him, so that, in desperation the "old doc" was sent for. I hurried to his bedside and examined him carefully. He was ill, there was no doubt of it, but not with appendicitis. The great specialist was wrong. The patient was the victim of a gastronomic ulcer; and his death would have been assured by an operation. I shuddered at the snap judgment of the city man, and leaving the house, ordered my neighbour to rest quietly. He died during the night—of acute appendicitis. I reached Chicago the next afternoon.

Once again the future looked hopeless. But once again my experience helped me. My imposing beard and knowledge of barn-cat anatomy pulled me to the top. I became assistant to a well-known veterinary, and by convincing him that powdered glass would kill worms, so destroyed his reputation that I succeeded in ousting him from his position. My superior knowledge and acuteness soon brought me fame— and a great deal of business. Cats, dogs, horses and goldfish—all have passed through my hands, into the great beyond. In this fashion did I retire, the St. Francis of medicine and the only man to fully understand the theory of sublatory osteopathy, Aesculapius, Hippocrates, Paré, Chamberlan—have any of them laboured for their generation as I have laboured for mine? To a grateful world I dedicate this auto-biography, secure in the knowledge that posterity will repay me in kind thoughts for what I gave her in skill, ability and honest hard work. I worked for the future; the future I know, will work for me.

---

# BORES
### By B. P. Mordy

"I REMEMBER back in '88 or was it '89 . . . . . "

When these words are heard in the reading-room of a club, all members know from bitter experience that the storm-signals are up for a three-hour monologue on tiger-shooting in Greenland, so they hasten to take cover behind the nearest newspapers and magazines. A queue immediately forms up outside the telephone booth as important calls with San Francisco managers are suddenly re-membered.

A new and unwary member may hear these words, and out of politeness will stay and listen, or try to listen. Poor man! Little does he know what he is in for! For the first fifteen minutes he suspects nothing, and is comfortable in his chair.

Then the intelligent expression which has adorned his face naturally so far becomes wooden; the lump in the chair padding becomes intolerable; and his mind wanders to other thoughts. After half an hour, the smile on his face becomes a painfully set grin. After an hour has passed, he is still outwardly calm, but inwardly he is delirious. His mouth automatically emits in a monotone the words "Yes, yes. How interesting!" at thirty-second intervals. This repetition becomes fainter and fainter. He slips lower and lower in his chair, drugged by some form of mental anaesthesia.

Fainter and fainter. Lower and lower. Fainter . . . and . . . fainter. Lower . . and . . .

Two hours later he is awakened by a hearty slap on the shoulder Automatically, he drools, "Yes, yes. How interesting!"

"You must come round to my house tomorrow, and I will show you the trophies I collected in Bechuanaland."

Needless to say, the invitation is never accepted. The new member goes on his way, a sadder and wiser man.

Then there is the fellow who is "reminded of a story." This brand of pest is, unfortunately, found almost everywhere in the "civilized" world. You will find him at cocktail parties, at Elks' Club luncheons, or at Government House receptions—in fact, anywhere that people congregate to talk.

At the first chance of an opening in the conversation he is "reminded." Then he is off. No one can stop the inexorable flood of words. For a few moments one seeks to escape in trying to think of yesterday's lunch menu, when he is brought back to earth by silence on the part of the narrator. He realizes with a start that at this point he is supposed to laugh. He tries to emit a polite guffaw but fails. The only result is a coarse, throaty cackle, and a mumbled "Haw, haw. That's a good one!" and the victim immediately sneaks off to distant parts before the speaker can be "reminded" again.

If the story-teller renders his effort in attempted dialect, then is the torture doubly unendurable. Then, the only thing left to do is to close one's eyes, take stern control of oneself, and think of the poor souls who died in the Inquisition. The man who finds a cure for this form of depravity will merit a Nobel Peace Prize, as well as the everlasting thanks of his fellow-men.

So far, only male bores have been dealt with; but do not think that women are innocent of this sin.

You all know the old girls who broadcast to the world the most intimate details of their illness and operations. Every tea or bridge party has its amateur diagnostician who is ready at the drop of a pin, or even less, to tell the assembled company what a terrible time she had with her sinus, or her heart, or both.

Strangely enough, her listeners hang raptly on every word.  But not because they are interested.  Oh, no!  That mustn't be expected.  Rather, they are watching, as a cat watches at a mouse's hole, for an opening in the spate of chatter which will enable them to cut in and babble about their own operations.  Thus, elderly matrons while away many a happy afternoon, revelling in the gory details of their own private, and oft imagined, ailments.

Add to these the woman who prattles endlessly about her riches; the man who pretends to know everything; and the people who forever talk on deep, obstruse subjects, and you have a fairly complete catalogue of bores.

However, it takes all kinds of people to make a world, so do not judge the bore too pitilessly.  Remember, you may be one too.

# THE LAUNCHING OF A SHIP
## By A. M. M. Curry

THE launching of a ship, especially a man-of-war, is a great event in any shipyard. She is the pride and joy of the men who have been engaged in the building of her so far, and their work must be perfect, for the hull must be light but very strong. They feel proud, for they know that the launching is the first stage in which they will see her grow from a gaunt, rusty skeleton to a live-bodied thing, ready to sail the seas on her lawful occasions.

The keel of the ship is laid on large wooden keel blocks which run horizontally to it. The bottom and the ribs are then attached and these are supported by large blocks of wood. All this takes place on the slipway, so that when the hull is complete a cradle may be built around it. This cradle is built underneath and around the ship so that finally it takes the place of the supporting wooden blocks. The cradle is prevented from sliding down the slipway into the water by large wooden shores which can be easily knocked away.

When the launching is ready to take place, a large wooden platform is built up in front of the stem of the ship. On this platform is a steel bar on a spring. The bar is at right angles to the bow which rises vertically in front of the platform so that when it is released it rises up and strikes the bow.

The launching ceremony is very impressive. On the end of the bar is held a bottle of Champagne dressed in red, white and blue ribbons. The bar is held down by a braided ribbon.

The sponsor of the ship first christens and then launches the ship. She says, "I name this ship ————, may God guide and guard all who sail in her." She then cuts the ribbon and the Champagne rises up and strikes the bow of the ship. The springing up of the bar starts off the mechanism which releases the last two shores, and the ship in its cradle slides backwards down the specially greased slipway into the sea.

The workmen cheer, whistles scream, and another ship has been safely launched.

# PURSUIT

## By R. W. Soper

A CROSS a large expanse of waste land, just above the timberline of northern Canada, a lone wolf galloped. Now and then he would stop and sniff the air, then, as if his life depended on it, he would throw up his head and howl; long and loud.

Once when he howled, there came back an answer. This could be barely heard, it was so faint, and far away, but it stirred the wolf to greater action, and he began to run with more vigour and he howled more often.

This animal was a monster of his race and he stood over two feet six inches at the shoulder. His coat was of a dark grey in colour and was very. thick for protection against the cold winter weather. Although the wolf was huge and well built he was terribly· thin and his ribs, as well as his hip bones and shoulder blades, were noticeably sticking out.

Ordinarily the beast would have slunk stealthily through the bushes which were scattered throughout the land; but now, he was running without any caution whatsoever, heading almost due east, and at each howl that he sent up, there were more and more answers which all seemed to get closer, as if they all were converging onto one spot.

Suddenly as the huge wolf topped a slight rise in the surface of the ground, he was met by half a dozen others of his race who immediately fell in behind him with a few welcoming barks, and then resumed the fast pace toward the east.

These six wolves, like their leader, were also thin and in dire need of food. They heard his cry and had instantly sent it on further and then had joined the pack.

Soon the six had grown to sixty in number, and more and more were joining them all the time.

Every wolf in the pack was half-starved, for none of them had so much as a bite of food for over ten days. Most of them were neither very old or very young, for the very old and the very young had either gone mad and been killed by their fellows, or they had died slowly of cold and starvation. Thus "the survival of the fittest."

Now the survivors were getting another chance to live, for several miles east of where the pack was running, a huge herd of caribou was moving slowly eastward. The heavy scent from their bodies slowly settling to the ground, left a perfect trail for the hunger-driven wolves to follow.

Soon the herd of caribou came to a small valley in a little range of unknown mountains where they were to spend the night. This valley was surrounded by large bushes which would afford good hiding places for anything attacking this group of unsuspecting creatures.

Sometime later the pack of wolves came upon the scene and immediately crept up under cover of the bushes. Then, with a howl from their leader they swept down into the valley, into the herd of startled and terrified caribou.

This was food; the lifeblood of all living things, the desire of the whole pack, and it was all here for the killing.

The leader dashed into the herd of plunging and kicking animals, and with a wild leap, he severed the jugular vein of a huge buck with a single, deadly, slash. Then turning, he left the stricken animal and made another terrific leap, driving his teeth into the leg of another young buck, successfully hamstringing him, and bringing him down.

Meanwhile the rest of the wolf pack was engaged in bringing down as many of the animals as possible before they became too scattered. The huge creatures screamed and kicked, as one by one they fell victims to the deadly tide of wolves, and one by one their screaming and kicking stopped, as with glazed eyes they slowly rolled over and died.

Soon the herd had been completely demolished, all of the beasts were strewn throughout the little valley, either dead or dying, with their deadly foes about them.

No sooner had the last Caribou been vanquished when a great howl arose from the pack: "The Howl of Victory."

.    .    .    .    .    .    .    .    .    .

Several days later, all that was left of a large herd of caribou was about a hundred skeletons scattered over the length of the little valley.

A few of the wolves still remained, picking the bones, and it could be seen that their coats were now sleek and that there were no bones sticking out or no ribs showing through their now fat sides.

Soon they left and the smaller animals took possession of the skeletons. A weasel flashed out from nowhere and began to pick uneasily at a rib of an unusually large buck. A fox came silently out of the bushes which surrounded the valley, and made his way delicately over to the half-eaten carcass of a luckless member of the herd and began to gnaw slowly on one of the vertebrae, meanwhile keeping a watchful eye on the weasel.

The pack of wolves split up and went their different ways. Their hunger had been satisfied for the time being and it would be some time before they would need food again.

The leader of the pack struck out for the west where he would have all the space he wanted, for he had no desire to be where there were forests, for he knew that where there were forests there were trappers and he had only one fear, Man.

The sun was setting as he started off for the great waste lands of the west.

———————

# THE WAY THE NAVY DOES IT
## By W. J. R. Edwards

WHEN you read of the glorious deeds of the battleships, the cruisers, and the destroyers of the British Navy, you are inclined to forget the lesser cogs in this wonderful machine. Yes, I mean the trawlers; those dirty, ancient, snub-bowed little boats that plough through the mountainous seas, the spray dashing in clouds of spume over their decks, searching, hunting, for the merciless U-boat.

The sea is not kind to the crews of the trawlers. They were born with salt water in their veins, and, as likely as not, when they die, the salt water will be their common grave. The dour British captain, his mate at his side, stands, leaning on the bridge-rail, and gazing far into the distance. The rain streams down their fine, weather-beaten faces, making them yet more leathery. The thoughts of the two men turn to their homes across the murky waves. They think of their wives and of their little ones.

Suddenly, there is a cry forward, "Torpedo off to port, amidships."

"Let her strike," shouted the captain.

There is a tremendous crash. The tiny ship lurches to port and begins to sink slowly, very slowly, to a watery grave.

The deck-houses "fall apart", disclosing wicked three-inch rapid firers, their gun crews by their sides, ready, waiting. Then the ominous grey conning tower of the Nazi U-boat breaks the surface.

"Fire," comes the order.

One of the deck-house guns belches death. A part of the conning tower and the periscope are blown away. A loud cheer is heard from the men on the trawler. The German crew pours onto the deck of the submarine. The fight is on in earnest now. A shell crashes through the belching funnel of the old trawler. The British guns are awash now, but the sweating, straining men ram home the breech to pump shot after shot into the Nazi sub. Waist deep in the water, the men still serve the guns, in an effort to get in the last shot.

Then, above the din, is shouted the order, "Abandon ship."

The rusty davits creak as the boats swing down into the grey North Atlantic.

The captain, who remains on the bridge, salutes, and then is seen no more. The cold waters of the sea have swallowed up another brave ship and another courageous captain of the Merchant Marine.

Lord Nelson's historic order: "England expects that every man this day shall do his duty", has been fulfilled once again.

---

# THE PROBLEMS THAT CONFRONT THE SERVICES

### Contributed by Lieut. W. H. Ellis, former Editor of the Ashburian.

AFTER fifteen months of this present war, a conflict in which the world has for the second time lost its head and, like a wilful child, set out to cause as much damage and grief as it knows how, it is perhaps fitting to pause for a moment to consider our present situation. Since September, 1939, the world has looked on as the one-time paper-hanger of Vienna has drawn more and more of the world into war such as has never before been known—a war of sudden smashing attacks, of shameless treachery, and of unnerving suspension.

From the point of view of the Empire, it has been, up to the present, a continuous battle for the supremacy of the seas and of the air. As yet, the armies of Britain and of the Dominions and Colonies, which are her buttresses, have been spared the Hell of a major land conflict. Of this we can be nothing other than fervently thankful, yet at the same time it must be borne in mind that the day will doubtless come when every last man of this great force will be used in the defeating of the enemy's might and in the final annihilation of those whose lust for power is the sole cause of our grief. Against that day there is being waged the greatest organizing campaign that the traditionally slow-thinking British race has ever undertaken.

At the close of what was then called "The Great War", there were stipulations laid down by the conquerors, to be observed by the conquered. Those stipulations were not severe enough, nor were they observed, and the net result is the chaotic cesspool in which we are immersed. Engaged in the struggle are the three chief services, the Navy, Militia, and the Air Force. Let us examine the task of each.

Since the Hundred Years' War, when England first earned for herself the name of "Mistress of the Seas", she and her ever-increasing possessions have had the task of maintaining free sea lanes for the trade routes which are their life-blood, a task equal to that of Sisyphus. The word "convoy," previously but a six-letter word in the dictionary, is now well known to every school child, and who has not read of the exploits of the Jervis Bay?

The fleet has a tremendous task. To begin with, it must be omnipresent. It must maintain supremacy in every sea at all times, and cannot for one moment afford to relax its vigilance. No chain is stronger than its weakest link, and, as was proved last May at Scdan, one break may spell utter disaster.

Again, the Navy must train men to handle the highly complicated mechanisms of its ships, a task in itself of no mean proportions. While the shipyards work feverishly to keep up the supply of vessels, the Naval Service must train men to handle those vessels.

During the Great War of 1914 to 1918, the habit of fighting from trenches became so prevalent that now we are inclined to forget that once armies never used those methods. The reason for the adoption of the trench system of fighting was that the effectiveness of newly developed weapons upon Infantry was so great that it was suicide to fight in the open. Now methods of fighting have again changed. Battles on land now take the form of vast encircling manoeuvres, carried out by all of the numerous arms of the modern army. But let it not be thought that only the Germans are capable of organizing parachute attacks, of using motor cycles and armoured fighting vehicles to advance fifty to sixty miles in one day. We, too, are quite capable of taking the initiative and sweeping before us everything that is part of the infernal Nazi or Fascisti machine  But that we cannot do until every part of our organization is complete and so thoroughly tested that there can be no failure. We cannot run the risk of a set-back. This then, is the answer to those fireside tacticians and beverage-room generals, who ask why we do not "Send our boys in there" to make an end of it all.

To-day we, in Canada, may wonder what is being done with the thousands of troops now in England. Very little of their activities is heard, and we are apt to forget about them. So far, this war has not placed the man-power of the Militia in the lime-light. After the Second Battle of Ypres, the Canadian Infantry was looked upon as *the* thing, and every youth who wished to serve in His Majesty's forces wanted to be an Infantryman. Now it is quite different. Little or nothing is heard of the Cavalry, Artillery, Engineers, Signals, Infantry, or of the many Services of the armed forces. Consequently, interest in them lags, and the result is that few youths long for the life of the foot-slogger. Gone is the glory of man-to-man combat—

lost in the excitement and surprise of the Blitzkrieg. Yet the day of the armies will come. It must come, for if it does not we are lost. No war has ever been won by passive defence alone. Nor can there be any decisive result unless the advances made by mechanical force.are exploited by supporting troops. Not one square mile of land can be held by machines, no matter how great their number.

With all this in mind, then, the British Empire is training millions of its sons in order that they may become proficient in the handling of their weapons, intelligent in their care of themselves against the enemy's cunning, and confident in the ability of themselves and of their comrades to reach their goal. For some reason, the armies of to-day are full of men of first class calibre, both mentally and physically. They are keen—keen to learn, keen to master the intricacies of the weapons which they must use both to defend themselves and to obliterate their enemy.

It has been noticed that of the recruits now being turned out at the Training Centres throughout Canada, there is a decided leaning toward the Air Force. On leaving the Training Centres, each youth is asked to state his preference amongst the three services, Naval, Militia, and Air Out of every ten, five give aviation as their choice.

Junior of the Services, the Air Force have proved to be of mettle as fine as any. Their part in this war is perhaps the most gruelling of a l. lCalled upon to make far more sorties than they would normally be expected to carry out, the pilots, observers, and air gunners are continually engaged in defending the bulwark of freedom, Britain. Night after night they soar aloft to meet the bombers and fighters that are part of Goering's Luftwaffe, who return night after night on their missions of death and destruction. Night after night the civilian army below cheers as the Royal Air Force sets out to give to Hitler's envoys of the air their just deserts.

And so it goes, with every man doing his utmost to attain the necessary efficiency with the minimum of delay. Throughout the Empire it is the same story. Bombing courses made the pupils of the Commonwealth Air Training Schools the best in the world. The British Navy trains its men so that performing their tasks perfectly is as natural to them as flying is to a bird. The Infantryman is trained until he is convinced that there is no sort of rough going that can stop him. The signalman is taught to be as resourceful as any spider. The Bren Gun is as well known to the soldier of six months' as is the automobile engine to the mechanic of six years' experience. Nothing is left for granted. Nothing is left untaught. The sailors, the soldiers, the airmen, are told why they are fighting or being trained to fight. They have it impressed upon them why victory is essential to the maintenance of the security of the world's weal.

# ABSENCE

*Oh, to have a little look*
*At England once again!*
*To walk once more*
*In London's streets*
*Or down a village lane;*
*To see anew the little house*
*In which I used to live.*
  *Oh, only just a little look,*
  *And anything I'd give!*

—D. NEGLEY FARSON.

# WITH THE ARMY IN PALESTINE

## By C. B. Pollock

THIS is an essay on coincidence. It is some time since the riots in Palestine were at their heat, so the order may not be exact.

The first one that I can think of is when a bomb made by the Jews was found by the police, and the Sappers of a very small division which had been stationed in Palestine came to the spot and blew it up. The bomb was a very good one, and where the destruction took place was approximately twelve miles east of Jaffa.

A week later an Arab saw the barrel part of a "flit gun." He thought that this might be another bomb, so he went to the nearest police station and notified the officer in charge as to where it was. All officials were notified and came to inspect it. Three shots were fired into it but it did not explode and it turned out to be just that, a "flit gun."

This story is told by a small boy called Fred Rice. At the start of the rioting we were in Ramleh, a short distance from Jaffa. One night, when Fred was sleeping, two very loud bangs woke us up. Fred's house had had two bombs sent through its roof. Fred's mother and father thought that it would be better if he went to Jerusalem, but that night the troops at the station sent up as many Very lights as they could, and that night was, for Fred, "the most terrifying night he ever had."

Finally we must record the near fate of Mrs. Goldsmith who was driving in the hills. She narrowly missed shots meant by the Arabs for a Police officer who had been stupid in his handling of the natives.

That was Palestine in 1937. The country is now temporarily united in its anxiety to win, with us, this horrible war.

*(This Essay was written by a boy of Abinger Hill School who is now with us and who was in the Holy Land at the time of the riots he describes. His father is District Commissioner in that most important town, Haifa, today.)*

| Name | Known As | Favourite Expression | Dedicated to Him | Hero | Weakness | Hobby | Ambition | Probable occupation |
|---|---|---|---|---|---|---|---|---|
| Andrews | Jack | Huh? | "Spicy Stories" | George Petty | Loaded Dice | Shooting craps | To be a "bad lad" | Curate |
| Bourget | Bob | (None of them very clever) | "Handbook of Civil Law in New France" | Stalin | Thurso and Nation Valley Railway | Crabbing | To blow up the school | Communist agitator |
| Conyers | Con | How about a quick one? | "How To Read" | Mortimer Snerd | His head | Having quick ones | None | None |
| Fisher | Pork | What sort of mood is he in? | "Little Lord Fountleroy" | Man Mountain Dean | His golf | Trying to hit a golf ball | To hit it | Still trying |
| Goodwin | Colonel | O.K. (See Conyers) | "Eleven more months and ten more days—" | Billy Rose | Moose Jaw, Sask. | Counting the days— | To take up where Billy Rose left off | Vet |
| Heath | Buzz | Yeah! | "A book of matches" | Bob Bowman | Near relative of preceding | Collecting cigarette boxes. | To get to the top | Printer's devil for the Citizen. |
| Lawrence | Barney | Lemme show you my new grip | "Ju-Jitsu In Ten Easy Lessons" | The name-sake in Arabia | (None, of course!) | Acting tough | To beat up Joe Louis | Thug |
| Lawson | Yank | I'll be back when hockey starts | "The Little Man who wasn't there" | Orville Burke | Yellow and black shoes | Wearing spats | "To flee the madding crowd—" | Hermit |
| MacGowan | Itzie | Shut up, Burrows! | "Down the Ice." | George Boucher | His skating | Yes, hockey | To crash the N.H.L. | Rink scraper at the Auditorium |
| McLaren I. | Jimmie | Oh, good lad! | "A Book of Latin Prose" | The Story book Man | Burgess's Bed-time Stories | Imitating people | To grow up | Shyster Lawyer |
| Neeld | Jack | Oh, yeah! | "Wessely's French Dictionary" | Paul Bunyan | His voice | Pitching hay | To be Fire Chief of Shawinigan Falls | Hired man on a farm |
| Peirce | Roy | —and, Ney, Stokowski told me— | "Shakespeare Five Tragedies" | Bill Sh-kespeare | That dreamy look | Playing the organ | The oracle of Coaticook | Hairdresser |
| Phillips | Dave | (Silence) | "Speech is silvern; silence golden." | William the Silent | Cricket | Sh! | ? | The silent service |
| Read | Oliver M., III | Now let ME explain this, Doctor— | "I Am an American" | Read | Uncle Sam | Guff | To outshine Marconi | Circus barker |
| Soper I | Walt | To Soper II:- Listen, you rat! | "My Merry Oldsmobile" | "Lucky" Teter | His coon coat | One-a-m driving | To outshine Capt. G. E. T. Eyston | Garbage truck driver |
| Thomas I. | Joe | Squad! on your markers Fall in!! | "The Pirate Airplane" | Santa Claus | Tinkertoys | Driving station-wagons that back-fire | Marshal of the R.A.F. | Patent medicine vendor |
| Wait | Scoop | Carry on, Canada! | "How to take a Photograph" | Walter Winchell | Talking about aeroplane engines | Stifling that eternal yawn | To conduct a dancing school | Janitor |
| Woodward I. | Charlie | He came Booming in— | (Nothing) | Douglas Fairbanks, Jr. | Pin-ball games | Hoping to hit the jack-pot | To marry Doris Duke | A male Barbara Hutton |

# THE
# ASHBURIAN
# JUNIOR
in which is incorporated

# ASHBURY COLLEGE
## OTTAWA

VOL. VIII        MICHAELMAS        No. 1
1940

*J. Hooper.*

# EDITORIAL

THIS issue of the Ashburian Junior incorporates in its pages the Abinger Hill magazine—for the duration. It was the unanimous opinion of the Editors that the Abinger magazine should not be allowed to lapse, because the School has taken temporary asylum over here. So until such time as the School returns to its own shores it is assured continuity in the pages of the Ashburian Junior.

But if this offer is considered a friendly and generous one—and we hope such will be the case—it carries with it too a certain obligation, and that obligation is this: the Abinger boys must be prepared to write for their new magazine, take an interest in it and see that its standard is not only maintained but, whenever possible, improved upon.

*"Tut, tut, child", said the Duchess,*
*"Everything's got a moral,*
*"if only you can find it."*

WE have often wondered in off moments what fun it would be if we could meet those people who no longer walk across our stage. How interesting it would be to meet Napoleon and ask him about the planting of the "flag bird" by the proud young ensign in the market place of Ratisbon. What a wealth of education would be gleaned from a meeting, say with Nelson, and hear him deny with his own lips the "Kiss me, Hardy" fable. And then, how fascinating it would be to meet and talk with such men as Robert Falcon Scott, Stephenson, Samuel Cunard, or Tom Edison.

All these men discovered something—Napoleon the wormwood of defeat after victory, Nelson that the greatness of a nation is the greatness of its people. Scott, our own personal hero, discovered the Great White South, Stephenson discovered the possibility of steam locomotion, Samuel Cunard foresaw the future of iron ships and vast trans-atlantic commerce. Our debt to Tom Edison is written wherever we turn the leaf to look.

But of all the great men of the past, all the finders, all the discoverers, nobody found anything of more lasting value than did Lewis Carroll. He found that the beauty of our language is a happy medium for wit; he discovered Alice. If he did not open up new lands in the physical sense, he did open up a new territory which our minds have never ceased to explore with superlative contentment for the last eighty years. The rudeness of the Caterpillar, the unhappiness of the Mock Turtle, the predicament of the Dormouse, and the mad scurryings of the White Rabbit, are a source of endless delight and the cause of infinite wonder. In its magnificent understatement, in its wit and humour, in its broad humanity, Alice in Wonderland stands in our library in a place by itself. We found and discovered Alice first when, in the words of A. A. Milne, we were very young. We hope to be still finding and discovering Alice when we are very old.

To those of you who, unlike ourselves, have not yet revelled in the delight of Alice's adventures, we recommend that you do so at once. With her, you too may walk through the Looking Glass into the land of pure fancy. In the pages of Lewis Carroll a world of fun awaits you, and your life will be that much happier for having sat down at the Mad Hatter's Tea Party. When you have read about that, when you have attended the Queen's croquet match, you will realize, we think, the great debt we owe that shy retiring man who signed his work Lewis Carroll.

The moral in Lewis Carroll—and he would have blushed to think that there was one—is the simple object lesson of kindness and humanity. The Duchess, though she searched everywhere, never found it, but we can if our minds as well as our eyes are open, on every page of Lewis Carroll.

# JUNIOR SCHOOL NOTES

W E Juniors welcome—and more than welcome -Mr. Harrison as Headmaster of the Junior School, and Georgina, too. We don't know which of the two we like the best.

Also, with a bit of fun in the matter, we hear that:

Matthews has spent most of this term in bed, although he seems to have still been able to keep up with the work.

"Battleship" Nelles, when playing rugger one day, was tackled roughly, and could hardly do anything strenuous for a week. He claimed to have scuttled himself.

Woods I has brought us two more of his kin this year, Shirley and Guthrie.

Arnould is putting abject fear into Nelles as he is rapidly swelling into a position to rival "Battleship's" weight supremacy.

MacNabb III (Charlie) has still not been able to get that chocolate bar from Mr. Sykes which he won from him in England.

Goodenough has had a very interesting time bleating at the Masters. We have, as yet, seen no horns sprouting.

Frost I does scarcely any work, but gets away with it—sometimes.

Gould, normally a brilliant scholar, has been experiencing some difficulty, we hear, with his Latin, but he is now getting better marks.

What's all this about the Hoopers not combing their hair? Can't be done.

Aunt Harriet and her teeth still present a problem to Turner.

And we have with us three gentlemen who speak for themselves—and how! Makovski, Tyrell-Beck and Parker.

Finally, to conclude the Junior School Notes, we hope that Mr. Sykes will have good hunting with the R A.F., if he goes back home next term. We wish you God speed, Sir.

# GAMES

## JUNIOR SCHOOL XI

### VERSUS ROCKCLIFFE PARK PUBLIC SCHOOL, WON, 1 - 0

O N Thursday, November 7th, the Rockcliffe Public School Soccer Team came to the Ashbury grounds to play the School.

Ashbury kicked off, and with this advantage managed to drive the ball to within twenty yards of the goal, but then a powerful kick by a Rockcliffe back sent the ball back to the centre line. Throughout the first half the ball kept moving back and forward, and there was no score.

In the second half, Rockcliffe got the ball almost to the goal-mouth where it was shot to the Ashbury left wing. Taken by surprise, the Rockcliffe forwards and half-backs could do nothing about it. Coming up the right wing, the ball was passed to Macnabb III, the centre forward, who shot, but the ball was stopped by a defence man. The left wing, seeing his chance, shot it in. No other goal was scored, making the final score 1 - 0 for Ashbury.

The line-up was as follows: Goal, Hamilton II; Backs, Mackintosh II, Eliot II; Half Backs, Thomas IV, Goodenough, Crabb; Forwards, Shinner I, West II, MacNabb III, Gould, Turner.

# THE WAGGLE

### (A Nonsense Poem)

The Waggle is a funny bird,
　He flits from tree to tree,
He feeds on jam and lemon curd—
　A funny sight to see.

You'll find his wings are made of lead—
　You'll find his head is, too—
You'll find his body's colored red—
　And his eyes are blue as blue.

He lives five miles from anywhere,
　In the middle of the wood;
He has a very comfy lair
　Like any Waggle should.

　　　.　.　.　.　.　.　.

This is the end of my little tale,
　Of the Waggle who lives in the wood;
Who eats his curd and jam in a pail—
　And a lot more than he should.

—M. W. SWITHINBANK.

# MY ESCAPE FROM FRANCE

### By P. Neumann

IT was on a cold, rainy Friday that we received the news of France's surrender to the Germans (whom the French called "les Boches"). My parents immediately left for Bordeaux, the only Atlantic port not yet taken by the enemy; but my aunt and I remained in the small village where we had our house. We all wanted to flee and escape the fate of our friends and relatives in Czecho-Slovakia. We were Czechs, and the Gestapo had our names written in their little books.

In order to go to Britain, it was necessary for us to obtain visas in our passports from the British consul at Bordeaux. But at this time young Frenchmen were pouring out of France to enlist in the Free French Army being formed in England. Naturally, they had to get their visas as soon as possible, so we had to wait.

We then planned to go to Lisbon, when my mother heard of a ship that had been chartered to transport Czechs from France to England. So with three small suit-cases and a small quantity of food, we embarked on our adventurous voyage. Our ship, the "Ville de Liège", was commanded by a Finnish captain. The "Ville de Liège" was an old Belgian ship which had been bought by American interests.

When we were about ten miles out of Bordeaux the French sent us word that it was too dangerous to attempt the crossing alone, so four more ships were sent out to us as a convoy. Our captain decided, however, that the ships should keep about three miles apart.

When we were two days out we received the news that Bordeaux had fallen into German hands. On the next day, we saw a very small French ship, also fleeing from Bordeaux. After about three weeks, during which we almost ran out of food, we reached Northern Ireland.

In peacetime the cross-channel trip could be made in an hour, but this was war. Because of German bombers in the air and German U-boats below the surface of the water, we had to steer a tortuous course. For the first week we headed straight out into the Atlantic, in the general direction of America, and then we sailed back to Belfast.

Here, our papers were checked by the military customs inspector, who informed us that we were lucky to be there, as all the other ships in the convoy had been lost, and presumably sunk.

Among those who accompanied us on this trip were thirty officers and men of the Czech infantry, who wanted to have another crack at the Germans, as well as five fliers in the Czech air force. I got to know them all, but my especial friend was one of the aviators.

After an uneventful crossing from Belfast to Liverpool, we took the train to London. We had reached our goal, and we were now freed from the dread of falling into enemy hands, and perhaps into a concentration camp.

*(The above is not a story, but a true account of the writer's actual evacuation from France.)*

D. Hooper.

# JUNIOR ART

### By J. M. Turner, Editor of The Ashburian Junior.

FOR two periods a week each form in the Junior School has a separate art class. These classes are taught by Mrs. Hunter, who was responsible for art last year. Form III, the highest form in the Junior School, is now doing designs. It has just finished a few paintings of flowers. By the end of the year, Form III is expecting to do some stencils, wall murals, patterns and linotypes. This year, on account of the increase in the Junior School, we may not be able to accomplish all of this, but we will have done well.

Most of the forms have done some painting or coloring and they have at least learnt something of the art.

The art classes this year are being held in the lab. instead of in the old art room. It is a very convenient place to work in and is well lighted. Art in the Junior School is a very interesting double period indeed.

---

# JACQUES CARTIER

### By A. Paish

CARTIER was a brave Frenchman who was sent to find new lands for France and a water passage to the East. In 1534 he sailed to Canada across the Atlantic Ocean. After a stormy passage he reached Chaleur Bay on the Gaspé coast and put up a cross there, claiming the land for France. The next year he came out again, but this time he went up the St. Lawrence River to the Indian villages of Hochelaga (now Montreal) and Stadacona (Quebec). He named the mountain above Hochelaga, Mont Royal, and he also named the St. Lawrence River. When he went back to France he took two Indian Chiefs back with him, and when they did not return five years later, when he came back to Canada again, there was some bad feeling between him and the Indians. After spending a bad winter, he returned to France for the last time.

# ADVERTISING
# SECTION

# MACDONALD'S

SINCE 1858

## We're Students Too

We've studied the apparel requirements
of youngfellows of all ages and are
prepared to meet their needs.

*Youngfellows' shop of*

# Henry Morgan & Co., Limited

*Colonial House, Montreal.*

*Students enjoy banking*

*at the*

# BANK OF MONTREAL

### ESTABLISHED 1817

*"a bank where small accounts are welcome"*

**THREE BRANCHES IN OTTAWA TO SERVE YOU**

Main Office, Sparks & Wellington Sts.
at O'connor St. · · W. R. CREIGHTON, Manager
Bank & Somerset Sts. · · · · · J. E. RIGGS, Manager
Rideau & Mosgrove Sts. · · · · B. J. CURRIE, Manager

*A MILLION DEPOSIT ACCOUNTS DENOTE CONFIDENCE*